MUMBAI TRAVEL GUIDE 2024/20

Explore the city's coastal charm, iconic landmarks and lively shores of Marine Drive.

Kimberly T. Akbar

Copyright © 2024 by Kimberly T. Akbar

All rights reserved. No part of this book may be reproduced, distributed, or transmitted in any form or by any means, including photocopying, recording, or other electronic or mechanical methods, without the prior written permission of the author, except in the case of brief quotations embodied in critical reviews and certain other non-commercial uses permitted by copyright law. Unauthorized use or distribution of this book, including any supplementary materials, will be pursued and prosecuted to the fullest extent permitted by law.

TABLE OF CONTENT

INTRODUCTION 5
   Brief Overview of Mumbai............................6
   Why Visit Mumbai?...8
   How To Use This Guide?...............................10
TRAVELING ESSENTIAL............................. 13
   Budgeting Your Trip..................................... 13
   Packing Essentials..18
   Weather And Best Time To Visit.................. 22
   Safety Tips... 25
   Local Customs and Etiquette...................... 27
WHERE TO STAY... 31
   Best Luxury Hotels...................................... 31
   Mid-Range Hotels..35
   Affordable Accommodations......................38
   Family-Friendly Accommodation...................41
NAVIGATING THE CITY................................. 47
SHOPPING IN MUMBAI.................................51
LANDMARKS & MONUMENTS..................... 57
   Gateway of India..57
   Chhatrapati Shivaji Maharaj........................ 61
   Marine Drive... 64
   Elephanta Caves.. 67
MUSEUMS & ART GALLERIES..................... 71
   Parks and Gardens......................................75
STREET FOOD AND LOCAL CUISINE..........81

    Local cuisine 81
    Recommended Restaurant 83
NIGHTLIFE & ENTERTAINMENT 87
    Bars, Pubs And Clubs 87
FESTIVALS AND EVENTS 93
    Theaters and Live Performances 97
    Beaches 103
    Trekking and Nature Trails 107
    Water Sports 107
DAY TRIPS FROM MUMBAI 113
    Elephanta Island 113
    Alibaug 116
    Lonavala and Khandala 120
ITINERARY 125
PRACTICAL TIPS FOR TRAVELERS 135
    Money and Currency 135
    Language and Communication 137
    Health and Medical Services 142
CONCLUSION 145

DIRECTION TO USE

- Install a QR Code Scanner App.
- Open the QR Code Scanner app.
- Position the QR code: Point your smartphone camera at the QR code you want to scan.
- Scan the QR codes: After successfully scanning the QR code, the app will often reveal the information within it.
- Follow the prompt and you're on your way.
- Otherwise, download your favorite map app and input addresses that are provided or names of places you wish to locate on the destination search bar and be sure to confirm your location. It will take you there from anywhere you're at.

Chapter 1.

INTRODUCTION

If you've ever imagined a city where the past and present coexist in a vibrant symphony, Mumbai is screaming your name. This handbook is more than simply a collection of recommendations and itineraries; it's your key to discovering the heart of one of the world's most vibrant cities.

Are you a first-time visitor or a seasoned tourist seeking for something new? Mumbai has a way of surprising you with its boundless energy, deep-rooted traditions, and unmistakable kindness.

You may be wondering, "What makes Mumbai so special?"

Consider this: ancient temples and bustling bazaars coexist alongside cutting-edge buildings and stylish eateries. It's a place where you may begin your day with a peaceful sunrise over the Arabian Sea and conclude it with a spectacular street celebration that overflows color and excitement into the night. The contrasts are what make Mumbai so unique.

But let's be practical—traveling to a city as large and diverse as Mumbai may be intimidating. That is where this guide comes in.

I wrote this book with the sole intention of making your journey easier, richer, and more pleasurable. Inside, you'll find everything you need, from the greatest locations to stay, eat, and buy to thorough itineraries tailored to all sorts of tourists.

Whether you're traveling alone, with family, or as a pair, I have you covered. However, this information is not limited to the popular tourist destinations. It's also about those off-the-beaten-path moments that give you a true sense of Mumbai's essence.

We'll visit local markets, obscure temples, and even a few secret cafés with cuisine as interesting as the stories behind it.

I want you to feel as if you're exploring the city with a friend who knows all of the best sites. So, are you prepared to begin on this adventure? Let this guide accompany you as you navigate the bustling streets, take in the sights and sounds, and fall in love with Mumbai's distinct charm. Trust me, by the end of this book, you'll be eager to pack your bags and begin exploring. Safe travels, and I will see you in Mumbai!

Brief Overview of Mumbai

Mumbai, often known as the City of Dreams, is a bustling metropolis in India where traditional customs and contemporary goals coexist peacefully. Here's a taste of what's in store for you:

Location: India's west coast, with an Arabian Sea view. 18.4 million people live in the Greater Mumbai Metropolitan Area. The official language of Marathi is spoken, along with Hindi, English, and a number of regional tongues.

Indian rupee (INR) is the currency.

Climate: Tropical monsoon, with distinct wet (June–September) and winter (December–February) seasons; hot and muggy for the majority of the year..

History

Ancient fishing settlements, a thriving British port city, and India's modern financial and cultural powerhouse form a fascinating tapestry. In 1661, England received Bombay from Portugal, marking a significant milestone.

Bombay became a prominent commercial city under British authority in 1818.

1947: India obtains independence, and Bombay is named the capital of Bombay State. Bombay is renamed Mumbai as Maharashtra gains statehood in 1960.

Twenty-first century: Mumbai develops into a global financial and technology hub. India's economy includes significant banks, stock exchanges, and Fortune 500 firms.

The economy is varied, comprising industries like banking, information technology, manufacturing, textiles, pharmaceuticals, healthcare, and tourism. The cost of living is expensive in comparison to other Indian cities.

Culture: A dynamic blend of Marathi, Hindi, and cosmopolitan influences. Bollywood, the world's largest film industry, is thriving here. Ancient cave temples and contemporary street art contribute to a rich artistic legacy.

Hinduism, Islam, Christianity, Buddhism, and Jainism are among the several religions practiced. Food: A wide variety of flavors, from spicy street food to international cuisine.

Why Visit Mumbai?

Why Mumbai, you ask? Imagine a city that is alive from sunrise to sunset, where every corner tells a tale and every street holds a secret waiting to be discovered. Mumbai is more than a destination; it is an experience, a maelstrom of sights, sounds, and flavors that will leave you breathless and wanting more.

Here's why: Mumbai is a city of contrasts, which is precisely what makes it so intriguing.

One moment, you're strolling through the old streets of the Colaba neighborhood, where colonial architecture stands tall, whispering tales of a bygone era. The next moment, you're caught up in Bandra's modern buzz, surrounded by chic stores and cafes that would seem right at home in any global city.

However, it is not only the city's diversity that makes it a must-see. It embodies Mumbai's spirit—its unwavering vitality, perseverance, and kindness. This is a place where dreams are realized, where millions come with hope in their hearts, and this spirit pervades every aspect of the city.

Whether you're riding a local train at rush hour or enjoying a calm evening on Marine Drive, you'll sense Mumbai's strong and steady heartbeat. Let us not forget the cuisine. Oh the cuisine! From legendary street delicacies like vada pav and pani puri to gourmet dining experiences in world-class restaurants, Mumbai is a foodie's delight.

Each bite is a voyage through the city's rich cultural fabric, which includes influences from all around India and beyond.

Finally, there are the people. Mumbaikars are a unique breed—hardworking, friendly, and always ready to grin. They will make you feel at ease, whether you are bargaining at a local market or getting lost in the city's streets.

So, why visit Mumbai? Because this city has a way of crawling under your skin and leaving an imprint on your heart that you'll remember long after you leave. It's a metropolis that never rests, never sleeps, and never ceases to amaze. Trust me, one visit and you'll be hooked for life..

How To Use This Guide?

Welcome to your perfect companion for visiting the vibrant city of Mumbai!

This guide is designed to make your experience as seamless and pleasurable as possible. Here's how to make the most of it:

QRcodes for directions

Install a QR Code Scanner App.

Open the QR Code Scanner app.

Position the QR code: Point your smartphone camera at the QR code you want to scan.

Scan the QR codes: After successfully scanning the QR code, the app will often reveal the information within it.

Follow the prompt and you're on your way.

Begin with what interests you

This handbook is designed to accommodate all types of travelers. Whether you're here for the history, the gastronomy, or the rich culture, you may go right to the portions that interest you. Use the Table of Contents to quickly find the information you need, whether it's a list of must-see attractions, hidden gems, or the greatest places to eat.

Prepare Your Itinerary

If you want an organized strategy, read through the suggested itineraries. These have been created to accommodate various travel styles, whether you're visiting for a weekend or a full week. The itineraries combine popular landmarks with lesser-known locations, providing a well-rounded perspective of Mumbai.

Useful Tips at Your Fingertips

Traveling to Mumbai can be an adventure in itself. That's why we've packed this guide with useful information, such as how to navigate the city's numerous modes of transit and how to keep safe and healthy. Look for parts on money, health, and safety to ensure you're prepared.

Get Into the Details

If you're a detail-oriented visitor, you'll like the extensive information on each destination, which includes historical background, cultural relevance, and insider recommendations. These insights can help you appreciate Mumbai beyond its surface, providing a more complete travel experience.

Bookmark your favorites

As you read, feel free to bookmark or take notes on the areas that are most useful to you. Whether it's a restaurant you can't wait to try or a cultural event you won't want to miss, this guide will help you plan and execute the ideal vacation.

Be flexible

While this guide covers all of Mumbai's attractions, keep in mind that the best travel experiences are frequently the result of unexpected discoveries. Use this itinerary as a starting point, but don't be afraid to deviate from the main road and explore the city at your own speed.

Connect to Mumbai's Heartbeat

Finally, this guide is more than simply a compilation of data; it invites you to engage with Mumbai's distinct soul. Read through the cultural insights, the history, and the local advice to properly appreciate what makes this place so distinct.

Allow this guide to inspire you to have an experience in Mumbai that is unique to you. Following these steps will prepare you to make the most of your time in Mumbai. So, take a cup of chai, settle in, and let us begin preparing your wonderful journey!

Chapter 2.

TRAVELING ESSENTIAL

Budgeting Your Trip

Traveling to Mumbai can be an exciting experience, but you must carefully prepare your budget to avoid overspending. Here's a comprehensive guide to navigating the costs and making sound financial decisions while enjoying everything Mumbai has to offer.

Understanding of Currency and Exchange Rates

Mumbai uses the Indian rupee (INR). Because exchange rates fluctuate, it is prudent to monitor the rates before exchanging your cash. ATMs are readily available, and the majority accept international cards. However, it is a good idea to keep some cash on hand, particularly in lower denominations, for local markets and smaller merchants.

Tip: Only use currency exchange services at reputed venues such as airports, banks, or official exchange facilities. To avoid scams, avoid street sellers who provide exchange services.

Transportation Costs

Mumbai has a diverse range of transportation alternatives, from affordable to expensive.

Local Trains: The local train system is the most economical option to travel vast distances within the city. A one-way ticket might cost between ₹5 and ₹50, depending on the distance.

Taxi and auto-rickshaws: Taxis (including app-based services such as Uber and Ola) are convenient, but they can be costly, particularly in heavy traffic. Auto-rickshaws are less expensive and better suited for shorter trips. Expect to pay between ₹20 and ₹200 depending on the distance.

buses: Buses are a cost-effective choice, with fares ranging from ₹10 to ₹50 based on distance and service.

Rental Car: Renting a car with a driver might provide additional freedom and cost between ₹1,500 and ₹3,000 per day. However, driving in Mumbai traffic might be difficult for people unfamiliar with the area.

Accommodation costs

Mumbai has lodging alternatives for all budgets.

Stay inside your budget: Hostels and inexpensive hotels cost ₹500 to ₹3,000 per night. These are ideal for solitary travelers and those on a small budget.

Middle-Range Hotels: Comfortable hotels with amenities like air conditioning, Wi-Fi, and breakfast typically cost between ₹3,000 and ₹7,000 per night.

Luxurious Hotels: Luxurious hotels in Mumbai range from ₹10,000 to ₹50,000 per night and provide exceptional services and amenities.

Tip: To receive the greatest rates and availability, book your accommodations ahead of time, particularly during peak tourist seasons.

Food and Dining

Mumbai is a foodie wonderland, with options ranging from street food to upscale dining.

Street Food: Street vendors offer meals ranging from ₹20 to ₹150. Don't skip local favorites like vada pav, pav bhaji, and pani puri.

Casual Dining: Casual restaurants typically charge between ₹300 and ₹1,000 per person.

Fine Dining: Fine dining in Mumbai typically costs between ₹2,000 and ₹10,000 per person, depending on the restaurant and menu.

Tip: Always check sanitary standards before eating street food. To assure freshness, go with popular vendors who have a high turnover rate.

Sightseeing and Activities

Many of Mumbai's attractions are either free or charge a little admission price, making it simple to tour the city on a budget.

Free Attractions: You can visit Marine Drive, Juhu Beach, and the Gateway of India for free.

Paid Attractions: Museums, historical sites, and other attractions often charge entry fees between ₹50 and ₹500. Foreign visitors should expect to pay approximately ₹500 to visit the Chhatrapati Shivaji Maharaj Vastu Sangrahalaya (previously the Prince of Wales Museum).

Guided Tour: Guided excursions typically cost from ₹1,000 to ₹5,000, depending on length and inclusions.

Shopping expenses

Mumbai has a diverse range of shopping options, from luxurious malls to lively street markets.

Street Markets: Bargain your way through markets like Colaba Causeway or Chor Bazaar, where you can get everything from clothing to souvenirs at low costs. Budget between ₹500 and ₹5,000, depending on your purchase.

Malls and boutiques: Set a budget of ₹1,000 to ₹10,000 on apparel, accessories, and home decor.

Luxury Shopping: High-end stores and boutiques in Bandra or South Mumbai might cost between ₹10,000 and ₹1,00,000, depending on your preferences.

Tip: Always bargain in street markets; it's expected and part of the experience. However, be respectful and know when to set a price.

Miscellaneous Costs

Tipping: Tipping is widespread in Mumbai, especially at restaurants and for services such as hotel personnel and cars. Tip 10% of the bill at meals and ₹50-₹200 for hotel and transportation services.

SIM card and internet: If you need mobile data, consider purchasing a local SIM card. Data plans range from ₹300 to ₹1,000, based on the amount of data and validity duration.

Health & Safety: Maintain a little budget to cover any unforeseen health or safety needs, such as over-the-counter medication, bottled water, or sanitizers.

Daily Budget Estimation

Budget Traveler: ₹2,000 to ₹5,000 per day

Mid-Range Traveler: ₹5,000 to ₹15,000 per day

Luxury Traveler: ₹15,000 or more per day

Tip: Always save aside some extra money for emergencies or unexpected needs. It's preferable to have a cushion than to be caught short. By properly managing your budget, you may experience all that Mumbai has to offer without breaking the bank.

Whether you're a budget-conscious traveler or looking to splurge, Mumbai has something for everyone.

Packing Essentials

When preparing for a trip to Mumbai, packing wisely might be the difference between a smooth, joyful holiday and one fraught with unneeded complications. Whether you're a lone explorer, a family tourist, or someone starting on a cultural journey, having the appropriate necessities will guarantee you're prepared for anything the city throws at you. Let us break it down:

1. Solo Travelers Are Prepared for Anything

Solo travelers must frequently pack with versatility in mind, ensuring that they can adapt to a number of scenarios, such as navigating congested streets, discovering hidden gems, or relaxing.

Essentials:

Choose lightweight luggage or backpack for easy transport and maneuverability.

A bag with secure compartments is perfect for keeping things nearby.

Travel-Sized Toiletries: Travel-sized versions of your necessities are compact and easy to store, which saves room.

Portable Charger: Mumbai is a lively city, and you'll want to document every moment.

A portable charger guarantees that your electronics remain powered.

Comfy Walking Shoes: Mumbai's streets are best explored on foot, therefore sturdy, comfy shoes are required. - Secure Travel Wallet: Protect your passport, credit cards, and cash with an RFID-enabled travel wallet.

Pro Tip:

Emergency Contact Information: Carry a physical backup of critical contacts in case your phone dies.

Small Padlock: Ideal for locking your backpack or for use in hostel lockers.

2. Family Travel: Fun and Functional

When traveling with family, especially youngsters, it's important to pack for efficiency and comfort while also being prepared for any unforeseen scenarios.

Essentials:

Family-Sized Toiletries: Sunscreen, hand sanitizer, and wet wipes are must-haves.

Snacks and Reusable Water Bottles: Keeping youngsters nourished and hydrated throughout the day helps reduce crankiness and keep everyone happy.

Entertainment for Kids: Bring a few small toys, novels, or a tablet loaded with movies and games to keep the kids entertained during travel or downtime.

First Aid Kit: Include basic supplies such as bandages, antiseptic wipes, and any prescription drugs.

Additional Clothing: Bring an additional set of clothes for everyone in your carry-on, especially if you're traveling with little children.

Stroller or Baby Carrier: If you're traveling with very young children, a lightweight, collapsible stroller or a comfy baby carrier might be really useful.

Pro Tip: Use packing cubes to organize outfits for each family member and find what you need quickly.

Collapsible Tote Bag: Ideal for transporting extras such as souvenirs, snacks, or emergency supplies on day trips.

3. Cultural Enthusiasts

Prepare to Explore and Engage: If you want to engage yourself in Mumbai's rich history and dynamic culture, make sure you pack for comfort and versatility.

Essentials:

Modest Clothing: Many cultural places in Mumbai require conservative attire. It is advised to wear lightweight, breathable clothing that covers the shoulders and knees.

Camera or smartphone with additional storage:

You'll want to capture the splendor of Mumbai's temples, markets, and ancient monuments.

Journal and Pen: For taking notes, reflecting, and even sketching scenes from your trip.

Guidebook or Travel applications: Using a detailed guidebook or applications that provide information about cultural attractions will improve your experience.

Hat and Sunglasses: Protect yourself from the sun during those long days of exploration.

Pro Tip: Use a scarf or shawl to cover oneself at sacred locations or as a light layer in cooler evenings.

Reusable Shopping Bag: Ideal for carrying products from local markets or for storing your guidebook and water bottle when exploring.

4. Adventure Seekers: Prepare for the Unexpected

Here's what you'll need if you want to explore Mumbai's wilder side, such as a trip through the adjacent Western Ghats or a day on Elephanta Island. Essentials for outdoor activities include lightweight, moisture-wicking apparel and good hiking shoes.

Daypack:

A small, comfortable backpack for transporting basics such as water, food, and sunscreen.

Insect Repellent: Especially useful for outdoor activities near water or in forested areas.

Waterproof Jacket: Mumbai's weather is unpredictable, especially during the monsoon season.

A portable water purifier or filtered bottle: Safe drinking water is not always easily available, so having your own filtering process is a good idea.

Pro Tip: Use a dry bag to protect devices and valuables from water damage during outdoor outings.

Compact binoculars: Ideal for birding or taking a closer look at faraway landmarks.

No matter what kind of traveler you are, packing wisely can improve your Mumbai journey.

Weather And Best Time To Visit

1. Summer (March-June)

Temperature range: 25°C to 40°C (77°F to 104°F).

Summer in Mumbai is hot and humid. This season is not suitable for anyone who is sensitive to high heat and humidity.

2. Monsoon (June-September)

Rainfall: Heavy rainfall, particularly in July and August.

Monsoons provide heavy rain and occasional flooding. Travelers who appreciate the monsoon ambiance and beautiful foliage may find this season intriguing, but expect inconveniences and damp conditions.

3. Post-Monsoon/Pre-Winter (October–February)

Temperature: 15°C-35°C (59°F-95°F)

Description: This is regarded as the finest time to visit Mumbai. The weather is more agreeable, with less humidity. It is appropriate for all types of travelers because it provides ideal circumstances for sightseeing, outdoor activities, and cultural encounters.

When is the best time to visit for different types of travelers?

1. Tourists and cultural enthusiasts:

Best time: October to February.

Reasoning: The post-monsoon/pre-winter season provides pleasant weather for visiting Mumbai's many historical monuments, museums, and cultural activities.

2. Adventure Seekers:

Best Season: Post-monsoon/pre-winter (October to February)

Reasoning: The weather around this time is ideal for outdoor activities like hiking, exploring national parks, and enjoying water sports along the shore.

3. Best time for festival enthusiasts is October-November (Diwali season).

Reasoning: During the Diwali celebration, Mumbai is alive with lights, decorations, and cultural activities. This period provides a distinct cultural experience.

4. Best time for budget travelers: monsoon season (June-September).

Reasoning: Accommodation and travel costs may be reduced during the monsoon season, making it an appealing alternative for budget-conscious vacationers. However, be prepared to face rain-related obstacles.

5. The best time for business travelers is the post-monsoon/pre-winter season (October-February).

Reasoning: The weather is pleasant, and the timing coincides with company calendars, making it ideal for business trips.

Tips for Travelers:

1. Pack As a result, wear light and breathable clothing in the summer, rain gear during the monsoon, and a mix of warm and cold apparel throughout the post-monsoon/pre-winter season.

2. Check Local Events: To maximize your cultural experience, organize your vacation around local festivals or events.

3. Stay Informed: Monitor weather forecasts, particularly during the monsoon season, to anticipate potential travel interruptions.

4. Hydrate: Due to the city's humidity, staying hydrated is crucial year-round.

Mumbai can provide a broad selection of experiences year-round by taking into account the distinct demands and tastes of various categories of travelers.

Safety Tips

Travel safety is critical in protecting tourists from potential hazards, resulting in a safe and happy journey

1. Ensure transportation safety by using reliable services like licensed taxis and ride-sharing apps.

   - Exercise caution when crossing roads; traffic can be heavy, and pedestrians should use marked crossings.

   - Use public transportation sensibly and keep your valuables safe, especially in crowded areas.

2. Personal Belongings: - Secure your belongings and be cautious of pickpockets in crowded areas, markets, and public transportation.

- Use anti-theft bags or pouches to protect valuable documents, money, and electronic gadgets.

3. Health Precautions: - Drink bottled or filtered water to prevent waterborne illnesses.

- Use mosquito repellent, particularly during the monsoon season, to avoid mosquito-borne diseases such as dengue and malaria.

4. Food and Hygiene: - Choose reputed and hygienic restaurants to minimize the danger of foodborne infections.

- Wash your hands on a regular basis, and keep hand sanitizer on hand in case soap and water are unavailable.

5. Cultural sensitivity: Respect local norms and traditions. Dress modestly, particularly when visiting religious sites.

- Avoid public shows of affection, which may be culturally improper in some locations.

6. Emergency Contacts: - Store local emergency numbers, including those of the nearest embassy or consulate, on your phone.

- Learn about the locations of hospitals and medical institutions.

7. Weather Preparedness: - Stay updated on weather conditions, especially during monsoon season. Be prepared for severe weather and possible difficulties.

8. Traffic and Pedestrian Safety: - Walk with caution on busy streets and use marked crossings.

   - Follow traffic laws when driving or taking public transportation.

9. Avoid scammers and touts, particularly in tourist areas. Avoid dealing with highly insistent people.

- Police: Dial 100 for police assistance.
- Ambulance: Dial 108 for ambulance services.
- Tourist Helpline: Dial 1800-22-3966 for tourist-related queries and assistance.

By following these safety precautions, you may ensure that your visit to Mumbai is both safe and enjoyable.

Local Customs and Etiquette

Mumbai, a melting pot of cultures and customs, greets you with open arms. Understanding and respecting local customs and etiquette is essential for making the most of your experience. Here's how to navigate the city's rich tapestry with grace:

Greetings and Body language

Namaste: The traditional greeting is to fold your hands together at your chest and say "Namaste." It may be accompanied by a small bow.

Head Nod: A simple nod with a grin is another typical greeting, particularly among younger generations.

Avoid physical contact: Handshakes are acceptable, but embracing and kissing should be avoided in public unless you are well acquainted.

Footwear: It is usual to remove shoes before visiting temples or homes. Look for approved spots to leave them.

Dress and appearance

Modesty: Dress modestly, particularly in religious settings. Cover your shoulders and knees, and avoid wearing exposed attire.

Respectful attire: When visiting government offices or attending formal functions, wear clean, modest clothing.

Footwear: Comfortable shoes are required for navigating Mumbai's streets. If you're visiting during the monsoon, wear sandals or sneakers.

Dinner Etiquette

Right-hand rule: In India, food is typically consumed with the right hand. Avoid using your left hand to eat or receive food.

Sharing is caring: Large dishes are often designed to be shared. Do not be startled if your dinner buddies offer you tastes of their cuisine.

Refusing gracefully: If you want to gently decline an offer, say "no, thank you" or "nahi, shukriya".

Social interactions

When addressing elders or those you do not know well, use titles such as Mr., Mrs., or Ms.

Personal space: Keep a reasonable distance during interactions, particularly with members of the opposing sex.

Avoid public shows of affection, such as hugging or kissing, as they may be deemed offensive in some communities.

Religious and Cultural Sites

Maintain silence and reverence at temples, mosques, and other religious sites.

Dress appropriately: Follow the dress guidelines for each religious location. Some may request that you cover your head or take off your shoes.

Photography: Always ask permission before photographing people, especially at holy institutions.

General Tips

Bargaining is common at marketplaces and with street sellers. Begin with a low price and bargain respectfully.

Gifts: If you're welcomed to someone's home, bring a small gift such as flowers or cookies.

Tipping: Tipping is optional but appreciated. It is usual to provide a little gratuity for good service.

Learn Basic Hindi: Knowing a few basic phrases, such as "thank you" (shukriya) and "please" (kripya), can be extremely beneficial.

Remember: Customs and etiquette may differ by community or location. Be aware and ask your local connections or guides about cultural subtleties.

Respect goes a long way. By displaying cultural sensitivity and kindness, you will get the respect and affection of the Mumbai residents.

Embracing these practices and manners will not only ensure a pleasant and respectful visit, but will also allow you to connect more deeply with Mumbai's dynamic spirit. So, broaden your horizons, enjoy the cultural tapestry, and let Mumbai's allure bloom before you!

Chapter 3.

WHERE TO STAY

Best Luxury Hotels

Mumbai is home to some of India's most luxury hotels, with world-class amenities, breathtaking vistas, and perfect service. Here's a fast introduction to the city's best luxury hotels, as well as all the practical information you'll need to organize your visit.

1. The Taj Mahal Palace in Mumbai

The Taj Mahal Palace is an iconic symbol of opulence, overlooking the Gateway of India and the Arabian Sea. It is noted for its history, elegance, and exceptional hospitality.

Address: Apollo Bandar, Colaba, Mumbai, Maharashtra 400001, India

Phone: +91 22 6665 3366

Room types include Heritage Rooms, Suites, and Presidential Suites. - Dining options include Wasabi by Morimoto and Sea Lounge. - Amenities include a spa, swimming pool, business center, and luxury boutiques.

Nearby attractions include the Gateway of India, Colaba Causeway, and Elephanta Caves (via ferry).

Prices range from ₹25,000 to ₹1,00,000 per night.

2. The St. Regis Mumbai

The St. Regis, known for its exquisite luxury, provides panoramic views of the city skyline and Arabian Sea. The hotel is popular among business travelers and celebrities.

Address: 462, Senapati Bapat Marg, Lower Parel, Mumbai, Maharashtra 400013, India

Phone: +91 22 6162 8000

The hotel offers deluxe rooms, suites, and presidential suites. Dining options include By the Mekong and Luna Nudo.

Amenities include Iridium Spa, outdoor pool, fitness center, and business services.

Nearby attractions include High Street Phoenix Mall, Haji Ali Dargah, and Nehru Planetarium. Prices range from ₹20,000 to ₹80,000 per night.

3. The Oberoi in Mumbai

The Oberoi, located in the heart of the city, is known for its refinement and individual service.

It also offers spectacular views of the Marine Drive promenade.

Address: Nariman Point, Mumbai, Maharashtra 400021, India

Phone: +91 22 6632 5757

The hotel offers luxury rooms, ocean view rooms, and executive suites. Dining options include Fenix, Ziya (Michelin-starred chef), and Vetro.

Amenities include a spa, fitness center, outdoor pool, and 24-hour business center.

Nearby attractions include Marine Drive, Chowpatty Beach, and Chhatrapati Shivaji Maharaj Vastu Sangrahalaya.

Price range: ₹18,000 to ₹60,000 per night.

4. The Leela Mumbai

The Leela, a peaceful sanctuary near the airport, offers elegance and traditional Indian hospitality. It is ideal for both business and pleasure travelers.

Address: Sahar Airport Road, Andheri - Kurla Rd, near Mumbai International Airport, Greater Indra Nagar, Andheri East, Mumbai, Maharashtra 400059, India

Phone: +91 22 6691 1234

Room types include Premier Rooms, Royal Club Rooms, and Suites.

The hotel has six dining options, including Jamavar and Citrus. Other amenities include a spa, pool, fitness center, and banquet spaces. Nearby attractions include Juhu Beach, ISKCON Temple, and Prithvi Theatre.Prices range from ₹12,000 to ₹50,000 each night.

Pro Tip:

Book luxury hotels in Mumbai ahead of time, especially during the high tourist season (November-February).

Make sure you book your stay in advance.

Airport Transfers: Most of these hotels provide free airport transfers to customers staying in suites or higher accommodation categories.

Check with the hotel when making your reservation. These hotels provide not only a place to stay, but also a complete experience of Mumbai's grandeur and beauty, ensuring that your vacation is both comfortable and unforgettable.

Mid-Range Hotels

The city also has a number of mid-range hotels that provide comfort, convenience, and affordability. Whether you're traveling for business or pleasure, these hotels offer great service and modern amenities without going over your budget.

1. Trident at Nariman Point

Trident Nariman Point overlooks the Arabian Sea and provides beautiful rooms, outstanding service, and convenient access to Mumbai's business and nightlife zones.

Address: CR 2 Nariman Point, Marine Dr, Mumbai, Maharashtra 400021, India

Phone: +91 22 6632 4343

Room types include Deluxe, Superior, and Suites.

Dining options include Frangipani and India Jones.

Amenities include an outdoor pool, fitness center, spa, and business center.

Prices range from ₹8,000 to ₹15,000.

2. The Ambassador Mumbai

The Ambassador, located on Marine Drive, is a popular choice for both visitors and business travelers due to its art deco decor and convenient location.

Address: Plot 7, Block 1, Veer Nariman Rd, Churchgate, Mumbai, Maharashtra 400020, India

Phone: +912222041131

Room types: Superior, Executive, and Suites

Dining options: The Society Restaurant and Flavors

Amenities: Rooftop restaurant, business center, free Wi-Fi, airport shuttle service.

Prices range from ₹6,000 to ₹10,000 per night.

3. The Shalimar Hotel

The Shalimar Hotel is popular among budget-conscious guests due to its modern amenities and convenient location in Kemps Corner.

Address: August Kranti Rd, Kemps Corner, Malabar Hill, Mumbai, Maharashtra 400036, India

Phone: +91 22 6664 1000

Room types include standard, deluxe, and suites.

Dining options include Gulmarg and The Bakerie.

Amenities include a fitness center, spa, free Wi-Fi, and meeting rooms.

Prices range from ₹5,000 to ₹9,000 per night.

4. The Residency Hotel Fort

This boutique hotel in Mumbai's commercial sector provides a comfortable stay with individualized care, making it ideal for both visitors and business travelers.

Address: Corner of, 26, Rustom Sidhwa Marg, Dr Dadabhai Naoroji Rd, Opp Citibank, Fort, Mumbai, Maharashtra 400001, India

Phone: +91 22 6667 0555

Room types include standard, deluxe, and executive rooms.

On-site restaurant serves Indian and foreign cuisine.

Amenities include free Wi-Fi, laundry service, tour desk, and airport shuttles.

Price range: ₹4,500 to ₹8,000 per night.

Pro Tip:

Book early. Mid-range hotels in Mumbai are frequently fully booked during high tourist seasons and festivals.

Booking a few weeks in advance can result in better rates and room availability.

The Airport Shuttle: Some mid-range hotels provide airport shuttle services for an additional fee or as part of a package deal. Make sure to inquire while booking.

Discover Local Eateries: While these hotels provide excellent eating alternatives, don't overlook Mumbai's famous street cuisine and local restaurants, which are frequently only a short walk away. These mid-range hotels strike the ideal blend between price and comfort, ensuring you have a comfortable and convenient stay in Mumbai without going over budget.

Affordable Accommodations

There are also choices of economical lodgings to suit budget-conscious guests. Whether you're a backpacker, a solitary traveler, or a family looking to explore the city without breaking the bank.

Here's a list of some of the top budget-friendly places to stay in the city:

1. YMCA International House

The YMCA International House provides clean and comfortable accommodations in the center of Mumbai.

This is a fantastic option for tourists looking for a safe and well-kept location to stay on a budget.

Address: International House, 18, YMCA Rd, Mumbai Central, Mumbai, Maharashtra 400008, India

Phone: +91 72089 28852

Room types include dormitories, single rooms, and double rooms.

Dining options include complimentary breakfast and an on-site cafeteria. Amenities include free Wi-Fi, gym, laundry service, and a shared lounge area.

Prices range from ₹1,500 to ₹3,500 per night.

2. Hotel Travellers Inn

Hotel Travellers Inn is a popular choice for backpackers and budget tourists due to its welcoming atmosphere and convenient location.

The motel provides minimal amenities at an inexpensive rate.

Address: 26, Adi Murzban Path, Ballard Estate, Fort, Mumbai, Maharashtra 400001, India

Phone: +91 1800 572 0709

Room types include single, double, and family rooms.

On-site restaurant offers Indian and Continental food. Amenities include free Wi-Fi, a 24-hour front desk, and airport shuttles (for an extra fee).

Price range: ₹1,000 to ₹3,000 per night.

3. The Backpacker Panda Colaba

The Backpacker Panda Colaba is a bustling hostel ideal for young visitors eager to meet new people and experience Mumbai's backpacking culture.

It offers both dormitory-style and individual rooms.

Address: 15, Walton Rd, Apollo Bandar, Colaba, Mumbai, Maharashtra 400001, India.

Phone: +91 96079 00992

Room types include mixed, female, and private rooms.

Dining options include shared kitchens and neighboring cafés.

Amenities include free Wi-Fi, lockers, laundry service, and a community lounge.

Prices range from ₹500 to ₹2,500 each night.

4. Hotel New Bengal

Conveniently located near Crawford Market, Hotel New Bengal offers affordable rooms with minimal amenities.

It's excellent for those who want to be in the thick of the activity without breaking the bank.

Address: 'B' Shalimar Estates, Sitaram Building, Dr. D. N. Road, Near Crawford Market, Mumbai, Maharashtra 400001, India.

Phone: +91 22 2340 1951

Room types include single, double, and triple rooms.

There are three restaurants on-site that serve Indian, Chinese, and Mughlai cuisine. Other amenities include free Wi-Fi, a tour desk, currency exchange, and room service.

Prices range from ₹2,000 to ₹4,000 per night.

These budget options ensure that your trip to Mumbai is both cost-effective and pleasurable, allowing you to engage in the city's rich culture without sacrificing comfort.

Family-Friendly Accommodation

Traveling with family necessitates lodgings that provide comfort, security, and convenience for all members, including youngsters.

Mumbai, with its varied choice of hotels, caters well for families looking for a relaxing vacation. Here are three family-friendly lodgings in Mumbai, each with features and services to help families have a great and stress-free holiday.

1. Taj Lands End

Taj Lands End is a stylish and pleasant hotel in the busy Bandra area. The hotel mixes modern conveniences with traditional Indian hospitality, making it ideal for families.

Address: B.J. Road, Bandstand Promenade, Bandra West, Mumbai, Maharashtra 400050, India

Phone: +91 22 6668 1234

Room types include family rooms and suites with extra beds accessible upon request.

On-site restaurants serve Indian, Continental, and Asian food, with kid-friendly menus.

Amenities include an outdoor swimming pool, children's play area, babysitting services, free Wi-Fi, a spa, and a wellness center.

Special family services include a children's activity center, family picnic packages, and babysitting (for an additional fee).

Prices range from ₹10,000 to ₹20,000 each night.

2. ITC Grand Central

ITC Grand Central combines old-world charm with modern luxury, making it an ideal choice for families seeking a calm and luxurious stay.

The hotel's big rooms and attentive amenities meet the demands of families with children.

Address: 287, Dr Baba Saheb Ambedkar Rd, Parel, Mumbai, Maharashtra 400012, India

Phone: +91 22 2410 1010

Available room types include family rooms, interconnecting rooms, and suites.

Dining: Variety of cuisines available, including children's meals.

Amenities: Indoor pool, children's play area, free Wi-Fi, fitness center, spa.

Nearby attractions include the Nehru Science Centre, Siddhivinayak Temple, and Phoenix Mall.

Special family services include babysitting, room amenities for children, and family-friendly activities.

Prices range from ₹8,000 to ₹18,000 per night.

3. Novotel Mumbai Juhu Beach

Novotel Mumbai Juhu Beach is a family-friendly hotel that offers breathtaking views of the Arabian Sea.

With immediate beach access, spacious rooms, and a variety of children's activities, it's ideal for families wishing to enjoy both the city and the sea.

Address: Balraj Sahni Rd, Juhu, Mumbai, Maharashtra 400049, India

Phone: +91 22 6693 4444

Room types include family rooms and suites with sea views.

The hotel offers a variety of restaurants, including kid-friendly ones, and 24-hour room service.

Other amenities include an outdoor swimming pool, children's play area, beach access, free Wi-Fi, fitness center, and spa.

Nearby attractions include Juhu Beach, Prithvi Theatre, and ISKCON Temple. Special family facilities include a kids' club, babysitting, a pool for youngsters, and beach activities.

Prices range from ₹7,000 to ₹15,000 per night.

Pro Tip for Families:

Kid-Friendly Menus: Ask the hotel about kid-friendly meal alternatives to ensure your children enjoy their meals.

Activities for Children: Look for hotels that have kids' clubs or play spaces to keep children amused during your stay.

Additional beds and cribs: Always confirm with the hotel whether extra beds or cribs are available if necessary.

These family-friendly lodgings strike the ideal balance between elegance, convenience, and fun, ensuring that everyone in the family, from the youngest to the oldest, has a memorable stay in Mumbai.

Chapter 4.

NAVIGATING THE CITY

Exploring Mumbai streets with local transportation, making it both thrilling and accessible. Whether you're taking a rickshaw, riding the metro, or enjoying the beauty of local trains, this book has all the practical information you need to easily traverse Mumbai.

Auto Rickshaws

Auto rickshaws, often known as "rickshaws," are an integral part of Mumbai's transportation system. They're ideal for short travels, particularly in the suburbs.

Where to Find Them:

Rickshaws are common in the suburbs, but are not permitted in South Mumbai (beyond Bandra). You may easily hail one on the street.

Always use the meter that starts at ₹23 (about $0.30). The fare increases with distance.

Payment: Keep small dollars or coins on hand because drivers frequently run out of change for larger denominations.

safety: For late-night travel, especially if you're unfamiliar with the area, it's a good idea to discuss your current location with someone you trust.

Mumbai Metro

The Mumbai Metro is contemporary, efficient, and an excellent way to avoid the city's gridlock.

Line 1 (Versova-Andheri-Ghatkopar) is currently functioning and connects significant regions in the western and central suburbs.

The metro is air-conditioned, on time, and suitable for people wishing to commute comfortably across the city.

Ticketing: Purchase tokens for individual travels or a smart card if you want to use the metro regularly.

Fares start at ₹10 (about $0.12).

Operating hours: The Metro runs from 5:30 a.m. to 11:30 p.m. Avoid peak hours (8:00 AM - 10:30 AM and 5:00 PM - 8:00 PM) for a less congested experience.

Security: Be prepared to undergo security inspections at all metro stops, including bag scanning.

Buses

BEST (Brihanmumbai Electric Supply and Transport) manages Mumbai's bus network, which covers almost the entire city and is an affordable option for long journeys.

Buses are a cost-effective method to experience Mumbai from a different angle. They are slower than other options but provide a more immersive view of the city.

Purchase your tickets from the onboard conductor. Fares range from ₹5-10 (about $0.06-$0.12), based on distance.

Apps: Use "m-Indicator" to find bus routes and times.

Comfort: Buses can become overcrowded during rush hours, so travel during off-peak hours if possible.

Taxis and Ride-Sharing

Taxis are widely available in Mumbai, including classic black-and-yellow cabs and app-based services such as Uber and Ola.

Taxis are useful for longer trips or when you have luggage. They provide a convenient and direct way to get to your destination.

Meter or App: Always request that the driver use the meter in traditional taxis, or arrange a journey using an app with fixed fares.

For increased security, especially at night, consider ride-sharing apps that track and share your trip with friends and family.

Local Trains

Local trains are the fastest means to travel great distances around Mumbai, notably between suburbs and the city center.

They are considered the city's lifeline.

Timing: Avoid taking local trains during peak hours (7:00 AM - 11:00 AM and 5:00 PM - 9:00 PM) to avoid crowds.

Women's Compartments: Female passengers can use ladies-only compartments for a safer and more comfortable journey.

Navigating Mumbai's intricate transit system may be difficult at first, but with these pointers, you'll soon find your way about this vibrant metropolis.

Chapter 5.

SHOPPING IN MUMBAI

Mumbai is a shopper's dream, with everything from lively street markets to opulent malls and trendy boutiques. If you're looking for one-of-a-kind mementos, the newest fashion trends, or simply want to soak up the city's vibrant vibe, shopping in Mumbai is an adventure in itself.

Here's a guide to the city's top shopping experiences, complete with useful information to assist you manage your retail adventure.

The Heart of Mumbai Shopping

1. Colaba Causeway Market

Colaba Causeway, one of Mumbai's most popular shopping destinations, offers a diverse range of products, including handmade jewelry, unusual home décor, and stylish clothing.

This crowded market is also an excellent place to purchase some souvenirs.

What to Expect:

A variety of vendors selling items from trinkets to fashion accessories.

Bargaining is essential, so improve your negotiation abilities.

Cafes and street food booths where you may relax and munch.

Location: Colaba Causeway, Colaba.

Opening hours: 10:00 a.m. to 9:00 p.m., daily.

Tips: Arrive early in the day to avoid crowds and receive the best deals.

2. Crawford Market (Mahatma Jyotiba Phule Mandai)

Located just a short walk from CST station, Crawford Market is one of Mumbai's oldest markets with a diverse selection of fruits, vegetables, and spices.

But that's not all; you'll also discover home things, toys, and pets, making it an intriguing location to visit.

Expect to find fresh produce, spices, and other food items at affordable pricing.

Sections for non-food items including kitchenware and stationery. - A lively, immersive encounter that provides a flavor of local life.

Location: Dhobi Talao, Chhatrapati Shivaji Terminus Area.

Opening hours: Monday through Saturday, 9:00 AM to 8:00 PM.

Tips:

Bring cash, as many stalls do not accept credit cards.

3. Fashion Street

Looking for affordable fashion?

Fashion Street is the place to go. This market, which has over 300 stalls, offers contemporary goods and accessories at low costs, making it popular with both locals and tourists.

What to Expect: Variety of wardrobe options, including trendy and casual styles. - Bargaining is essential—prices can often be drastically reduced.

Quick street food alternatives nearby for a snack break.

Location: MG Road, South Mumbai.

Opening hours: 11:00 a.m. to 8:00 p.m., daily.

Tips:

Fitting rooms are limited, so be prepared to try on garments over your own.

Luxury Shopping with Style

1. High Street Phoenix & Palladium.

For those who prefer a more refined setting, High Street Phoenix and the nearby Palladium Mall provide a high-end shopping experience. Luxury brands can be found alongside prominent foreign and Indian ones.

Expect a diverse range of boutiques, including Zara, H&M, and luxury labels such as Gucci and Jimmy Choo.

Dining options vary from modest cafes to upmarket restaurants.

Regular events, fashion displays, and exhibitions enhance the shopping experience.

Location: Lower Parel

Opening Hours: 11:00 AM to 10:00 PM daily.

Tips: Visit during the week to avoid weekend crowds.

2. Phoenix Marketcity

Located in Kurla, Phoenix Marketcity is one of Mumbai's largest malls, featuring a mix of high-street goods, entertainment, and food. It serves as a one-stop shop, eat, and play destination.

What to Expect:

A diverse range of fashion, electronics, and lifestyle stores.

Multiplex theaters, gaming arcades, and other entertainment opportunities.

Food courts and fine dining options include a variety of cuisines.

Location: LBS Marg, Kurla West

Opening Hours: 11:00 AM to 10:00 PM daily.

Tip: Check out their seasonal sales for excellent deals.

Unique Finds and Designer Labels

1. Kala Ghoda stores

The Kala Ghoda region is noted for its creative vibe, which the stores reflect. Shopping at Kala Ghoda is all about finding something special and distinctive, whether it's handcrafted jewelry or luxury goods.

What to Expect:

Boutiques with unique, handcrafted items ideal for giving.

An opportunity to discover rising Indian designers and artisans.

The neighborhood also has art galleries and cafes, so it's a nice place to spend the afternoon.

Location: Kala Ghoda, Fort.

Operating Hours: 10:00 AM - 7:00 PM, Monday through Saturday.

Tips: While shopping, take the opportunity to check out the local street art and galleries.

2. Bandra stores

Bandra is recognized for its fashionable ambiance, with stores offering a mix of high fashion and unusual finds. Whether you're seeking for the latest Indian fashion or one-of-a-kind home décor, Bandra's stores will not disappoint.

What to Expect: A mix of high-end designer stores and unique independent boutiques.

Fashion-forward clothing, accessories, and home decor.

A youthful, fashionable vibe with numerous cafes and street art.

Location: Linking Road, Hill Road, Bandra West.

Opening hours: 11:00 a.m. to 8:00 p.m., daily.

Tips: Take a rest in one of Bandra's numerous cafés or street food carts.

Mumbai offers a shopping experience unlike any other. Whether you're browsing the colorful markets of Colaba and Crawford, indulging in retail therapy at the luxury malls of Lower Parel, or looking for one-of-a-kind finds in the fashionable shops of Kala Ghoda and Bandra, this dynamic city has something for individuals.

Chapter 6

LANDMARKS & MONUMENTS

Gateway of India

Seeing the Gateway of India for the first time, it freezes you in your tracks. Perhaps it's the way the arch stretches for the sky or frames the limitless horizon of the Arabian Sea.

But there's more than just a physical presence here—a visceral energy that speaks to Mumbai's soul.

As you stand in front of this massive archway, you are more than just a tourist admiring a piece of history; you are part of a live story.

The Gateway of India, built in 1924 to honor the arrival of British royalty, has seen the ebb and flow of history, from the grandeur of the British Raj to the dawn of India's freedom.

It has witnessed joyful celebrations, tearful farewells, and everything in-between. And now it welcomes you. But what actually distinguishes the Gateway of India is not merely its history or architecture, though both are unquestionably spectacular. It is how it makes you feel.

Location: Apollo Bunder, Colaba, Mumbai.

Time of operation

The Gateway of India is open from 7:00 AM to 5:00 PM every day.

Entry Fee

Entry to the Gateway of India is free. However, there are expenses for some activities, such as boarding a ferry or visiting the Taj Mahal Palace.

Sightseeing

Admire the architecture: The Gateway of India is an Indo-Saracenic architectural marvel that combines Indian, Muslim, and European elements. Admire the elaborate masonry, towering arch, and basalt-faced piers.

Enjoy the waterfront view: Stroll along the coastline and take in the spectacular views of the Arabian Sea. You can also take a ferry from the Gateway to Elephanta Island or other neighboring destinations.

Visit the Taj Mahal Palace. The renowned Taj Mahal Palace hotel is situated directly adjacent to the Gateway of India.

Take a stroll through the opulent lobby or dine at one of the hotel's restaurants with spectacular sea views.

Explore the National Museum. The Chhatrapati Shivaji Maharaj Vastu Sangrahalaya, better known as the Prince of Wales Museum, is just a short walk from the Gateway of India. This large museum exhibits an extensive collection of relics from India's rich history and culture.

Activities

Take a picturesque ferry trip from the Gateway to Elephanta Island, a UNESCO World Heritage Site including ancient cave temples.

Hire a private boat to explore Mumbai's port, passing past prominent locations such as Marine Drive and the Taj Mahal Palace.

A traditional horse-drawn carriage ride along the waterfront provides a unique and romantic experience.

Have a picnic. Bring a picnic lunch and enjoy the outdoors on the grassy grounds near the Gateway.

Shop for souvenirs: Peruse the stalls of local vendors selling souvenirs, handicrafts, and spices.

Additional tips:

The best time to visit the Gateway of India is in the early morning or late evening to avoid crowds and enjoy the nice weather.

There will be some walking involved, wearing comfortable shoes.

Be mindful of your possessions and take safeguards against petty theft.

Bring a water bottle and sunscreen, especially if you are visiting during the daytime.

In this never-stopping metropolis, you'll learn that the Gateway of India is more than simply a landmark; it's Mumbai's heartbeat.

And for those who have felt its pulse, it is a place that sticks with you long after you leave, beckoning you back time and again. So, when you think about Mumbai, consider the Gateway not just as a place, but as an experience—a feeling that you'll take with you wherever you go.

Chhatrapati Shivaji Maharaj

Chhatrapati Shivaji Maharaj is one of the most respected figures in Indian history, noted for his bravery, strategic brilliance, and leadership abilities.

As the founder of the Maratha Empire in western India in the 17th century, he was instrumental in fighting Mughal expansion and building a domain founded on justice and government.

His legacy and contributions to Indian history made him a popular figure among both locals and visitors visiting Maharashtra.

Getting There

By train: As a railway terminus, CST is easily accessible by train from various regions of India. You can purchase tickets online or at the station.

Taxis and cabs are widely accessible outside the station. Ride-hailing apps such as Ola and Uber are also available in Mumbai.

By bus: Several BEST buses travel to and from CST. You may look up bus routes and times online or at the stations.

By metro: The closest metro station is Church gate, which is a 10-minute walk from CST.

Address

Chhatrapati Shivaji Maharaj Terminus Area, Fort, Mumbai, Maharashtra 400001, India.

Sightseeing

CST, a UNESCO World Heritage Site, is known for its stunning Indo-Gothic architecture.

The station features stunning carvings, stained glass windows, and a magnificent dome.

The Central Hall is the heart of the station, with a mosaic floor, lofty ceilings, and huge chandeliers.

The Chhatrapati Shivaji Maharaj Museum, located within the station, showcases the history of Indian railways.

The station bookstore has a selection of books on Indian history, culture, and trains. There is no entrance fee to visit the Chhatrapati Shivaji Terminus. However, there is a nominal fee to see the museum.

Opening hours

The station is open 24 hours a day, seven days a week. However, some businesses and eateries within the station may have specified opening and closing times.

Activities

Take a heritage walk: Several tour companies provide guided heritage walks through CST that tell you about the station's history and design. Enjoy a meal: The station features a variety of eateries and cafes serving Indian and international cuisine. People-watching: CST is a thriving hub of activity, and people-watching is a great way to learn about the local culture.

Station stores provide mementos such as keychains, magnets, and postcards.

Best Time to Visit: CSMT is open to the public all year round, but the best time to visit is early morning or late evening when the station is less crowded, and the lighting highlights the architectural details beautifully. Guided tours are available if you want a deeper understanding of its history and significance.

Entrance Fee: There is no entrance fee to enter the station itself. However, if you're interested in exploring the heritage gallery inside the terminus, a small fee is charged.

Marine Drive

Marine Drive, also known as the "Queen's Necklace," is one of Mumbai's most recognizable and beloved monuments.

This wide arc of a road, bordered with palm palms and running beside the Arabian Sea, provides spectacular views of the ocean, particularly around sunset.

By night, the streetlights that curl around the bay resemble a string of pearls, earning the promenade its moniker.

What to See and Do on Marine Drive

1. Sunset Views: The most popular times to visit Marine Drive are in the late afternoon and early evening. As the sun sinks below the horizon, the sky explodes in hues of orange, pink, and purple, reflecting magnificently on the Arabian Sea. It's a breathtaking sight that entices both locals and tourists to sit on the sea-facing promenade and take in the scenery.

2. Chowpatty Beach: Chowpatty Beach, located at the northern end of Marine Drive, is a popular destination for street food vendors and a celebratory environment.

You may eat Mumbai's famed delicacies, such as pav bhaji, bhel puri, and pani puri, while taking in the cool sea wind. The beach is also ideal for an evening stroll or simply observing the people relax after a long day.

3. Walk down the promenade.

Walking the 3.6-kilometer stretch of Marine Drive is an experience in and of itself. The promenade is spacious and clean, making it suitable for a leisurely stroll, running, or cycling.

Along the route, you'll see couples admiring the scenery, families going for a walk, and street performers contributing to the lively ambiance.

4. Architectural marvels: Marine Drive is surrounded with Art Deco structures from the 1930s and 1940s. These structures, with their distinct style, add to the area's old-world appeal.

The region between Nariman Point to Chowpatty Beach contains the world's second-largest concentration of Art Deco buildings, behind Miami. If you enjoy architecture, a walk around this region is a must.

5. Nariman Point: Nariman Point, Mumbai's premier business zone, is located on the southern end of Marine Drive. From here, you can take in panoramic views of the Arabian Sea and the skyline. It's also a nice place to

sit and watch the waves crash against the rocks, or to get a coffee at one of the neighboring cafes.

How To Get There

Marine Drive is well-connected to Mumbai's public transportation system.

You can take a taxi, bus, or local train.

The nearest train stations are Churchgate (Western Line) and Marine Lines (Western Line), which are both a short walk from the promenade.

When is the best time to visit?

The best time to visit Marine Drive is late afternoon or evening, especially if you want to see the sunset. However, early mornings are also calm, with fewer people and a quieter atmosphere.

It's a free attraction that provides one of the most memorable experiences in Mumbai.

Safety Tip

Marine Drive is relatively safe, but like with any tourist destination, it's best to be wary of your things, especially in crowded areas. The neighborhood is well-lit at night, making it suitable for nighttime strolls.

Elephanta Caves

The Elephanta Caves, a UNESCO World Heritage Site, provide an intriguing look into Mumbai's ancient history and rich cultural heritage.

These rock-cut caverns, located on Elephanta Island in the Arabian Sea, some ten kilometers east of Mumbai, date from the fifth to seventh century and are largely dedicated to the Hindu god Shiva.

Exploring The Elephanta Caves

1. The Main Cave (Cave 1) Cave 1, also known as the Great Cave, is the most significant and expansive of the caverns.

As you enter, you are met by towering pillars and beautiful rock carvings that demonstrate ancient India's architectural brilliance.

The colossal 20-foot-tall statue of the three-headed Shiva, known as "Trimurti," serves as the cave's centerpiece.

This magnificent artwork depicts Shiva in his three forms: Creator, Preserver, and Destroyer.

2. Sculptures: The caves are embellished with amazing sculptures of many forms of Shiva.

These contain scenes of Shiva as Nataraja, the Lord of Dance, as well as the heartfelt moment of his marriage with Parvati. Despite decades of degradation, the attention to detail in these sculptures reflects the artistry of those who chiseled them from the hard basalt rock.

3. Other Caves: In addition to the main cave, there are other smaller caverns spread throughout the island, each with its own distinct carvings and historical significance.

While not as grand as the Great Cave, these caverns provide a more peaceful setting to contemplate on the island's spiritual and cultural past.

4. Panoramic Views: After visiting the caves, walk to the summit of the island for breathtaking panoramic views of Mumbai's cityscape and the huge Arabian Sea.

The lush flora that surrounds the island contributes to the sense of tranquility and provides an excellent contrast to Mumbai's hectic lifestyle.

Location: Elephanta Island is about ten kilometers east of Mumbai in the Arabian Sea.

How To Get There

The Elephanta Caves can be reached by ferry from the Gateway of India in Mumbai. The ferry voyage takes approximately 1 to 1.5 hours each way and provides stunning views of the city's waterfront.

Ferries run frequently throughout the day, so it's best to start your journey early to avoid congestion.

Entrance Fees

There is an entrance fee for entering the caves.

The cost for foreign tourists is typically ₹600 (approximately $7.50 USD), while Indian nationals pay ₹40 (approximately $0.50 USD).

Photography and filming may require an additional cost.

Timetable: The caves are open daily from 9:00 a.m. to 5:30 p.m., except on Mondays, when they are closed to tourists.

When is the best time to visit?

The greatest time to visit the Elephanta Caves is from November to February, when the weather is milder and more pleasant.

Avoid visiting during the monsoon season (June-September), as ferry services may be affected owing to strong waves.

What to bring: There will be a lot of walking and climbing, so comfortable walking shoes are essential. It is also suggested to bring water, a hat, and sunscreen because the island may get fairly hot during the day.

Guided Tour: Those interested in the caverns' history and features should hire a local guide. Guides are available for hiring at the cave entrance and can provide additional information on the sculptures and the island's history.

The Elephanta Caves are more than just a tourist attraction; they represent a trip through India's spiritual and creative past.

As you walk through these ancient rock-cut temples, you'll feel a strong connection to the history, mythology, and artistry that have helped build Mumbai into the bustling metropolis it is today.

Chapter 7

MUSEUMS & ART GALLERIES

Mumbai, has an extensive array of museums and art galleries that highlight the city's diversified heritage, dynamic history, and thriving arts scene.

From historical relics to contemporary art, these cultural institutions provide an in-depth look into the city's essence.

1. Chhatrapati Shivaji Maharaj Vastu Sangrahalaya (CSMVS). CSMVS, formerly known as the Prince of Wales Museum, is Mumbai's premier museum, housing an extensive collection of items from India's history, such as sculptures, paintings, and decorative arts.

Highlights include ancient sculptures from the Indus Valley Civilization.

Miniature paintings from various parts of India.

A collection of European and Asian weapons and armor.

Location: Kala Ghoda, Fort, Mumbai.

Opening Hours: 10:15 AM to 6:00 PM (closed on Mondays).

The entry fee is ₹85 (about. $1) for Indian citizens and ₹500 (approx. $6) for international nationals.

Photography: Allowed for an extra charge.

The nearest railway stations are Churchgate (Western Line) and CST (Central Line).

2. The National Gallery of Modern Art (NGMA).

The NGMA is a must-see for art lovers, exhibiting contemporary Indian art from the mid-nineteenth century to the present.

The gallery features rotating exhibitions of works by notable Indian artists such as Raja Ravi Varma, M.F. Husain, and F.N. Souza.

Highlights:

Rotating exhibitions with contemporary Indian and foreign artists.

A permanent collection of works by Indian modern art pioneers.

Workshops and guided tours to gain a better knowledge of the displays.

Location: Sir Cowasji Jahangir Public Hall on MG Road in Fort, Mumbai.

Hours: Open daily from 11:00 AM to 6:00 PM (closed Mondays).

The entry fee is ₹20 (about. $0.25) for Indian citizens and ₹500 (approx. $6) for international nationals.

Photography is not permitted within the galleries.

The nearest train stations are Churchgate and CST.

3.Dr. Bhau Daji Lad Museum

Dr. Bhau Daji Lad Museum, Mumbai's oldest museum, provides a fascinating peek into the city's history with its amazing collection of ornamental arts, textiles, and historical pictures.

The museum frequently holds exhibitions and cultural events.

Highlights:

Dioramas show Mumbai's transformation from a fishing town to a bustling metropolis.

Displays Indian ceramics, textiles, and maps.

Organizes cultural events and exhibitions.

Location: 91A, Rani Baug, Byculla East, Mumbai. - Open Hours: 10:00 AM to 6:00 PM (closed on Wednesdays).

The entry fee is ₹10 (about. $0.15) for Indian citizens and ₹100 (approx. $1.25) for foreign nationals.

Photography: Allowed for an extra charge.

4. Jehangir Art Gallery

Jehangir Art Gallery, located in Mumbai's cultural neighborhood of Kala Ghoda, is one of the city's most notable contemporary art locations.

The gallery frequently holds shows by emerging and established artists, making it a vibrant location for art enthusiasts.

Highlights:

Regular exhibitions of works by local and foreign artists.

A valuable forum for budding Indian artists.

Located in the busy Kala Ghoda neighborhood, which is recognized for its art and culture scene. Location: 161B, Mahatma Gandhi Road, Kala Ghoda, Fort, Mumbai.

Opening hours: 11:00 a.m. to 7:00 p.m.

Free admission.

Photography: allowed.

These museums and art galleries in Mumbai provide a glimpse into the city's rich cultural landscape, ranging from ancient history to present artistic expression. Whether you're an art enthusiast, history buff, or simply a curious traveler, these cultural institutions will give you a better knowledge and respect for Mumbai's distinct legacy.

Parks and Gardens

A Green Retreat in the City Mumbai, known for its fast-paced lifestyle, also has peaceful green places where residents and visitors can relax. Here's a guide to some of Mumbai's top parks and gardens.

1. Sanjay Gandhi National Park

SGNP, spanning over 104 square kilometers, is one of the world's largest urban parks. Located in the northern section of Mumbai, it is a nature lover's paradise, with a diverse range of flora and fauna.

What to Do:

Kanheri caverns: Explore these ancient Buddhist caverns from the 1st century BCE.

Nature routes: Several routes allow for leisurely excursions, which are ideal for bird watching and wildlife viewing.

Boat Rides: Take a relaxing boat ride on the park's lake.

Opening hours are 7:30 a.m. to 6:30 p.m. daily.

Entry fee is ₹58 for adults (about $0.70) and ₹31 for children (around $0.40).

The Best Time to Visit: Early morning or late afternoon to escape the heat and see the animals at its most active.

How to Get There: Easily accessible by train from Borivali station. From there, take a short rickshaw ride to the park's entrance.

2. Hanging Gardens (Pherozeshah Mehta Gardens)

Situated atop Malabar Hill, the Hanging Gardens provide breathtaking views of the Arabian Sea and Marine Drive.

The garden is well-known for its well groomed hedges styled like animals, making it a popular family destination.

How to Proceed: Relax and unwind by strolling through the grounds and taking in the gorgeous views.

Photography: Capture the sunset over the sea, which is one of Mumbai's most picturesque landscapes.

Opening hours are 5:00 AM to 9:00 PM daily.

Entrance Fee: Free.

The best time to visit is in the early evening to witness the sunset.

How To Get There: The closest train station is Charni Road, from where you can catch a taxi or rickshaw.

3. Kamala Nehru Park

Located near the Hanging Gardens, Kamala Nehru Park is a famous destination on Malabar Hill. It is well known for its huge shoe structure, which is popular with youngsters, but it also provides panoramic views of the city.

How to Proceed:

Children's Play Area: A terrific place for kids to play and explore the iconic "Old Woman's Shoe" structure.

Viewpoints: Admire the expansive views of Marine Drive and the Queen's Necklace.

Opening hours are 5:00 AM to 9:00 PM daily.

Entrance Fee: Free.

The best time to visit:

Late afternoon or early evening.

How To Get There: Close to the Hanging Gardens, Charni Road is the nearest train station.

4. Shivaji Park

Shivaji Park, located in Dadar, is one of Mumbai's major public areas. It's a popular spot for cricket fans and political events, flanked by residential structures and local restaurants.

What to Do:

Cricket Matches: Attend local cricket games in this park, where many great Indian cricketers, such as Sachin Tendulkar, began their careers.

Morning Walks: Perfect for an early-morning jog or walk.

Opening Hours: Available 24 hours.

Entrance Fee: Free.

How To Get There: The nearest train stations are Dadar and Matunga. Both are a short walk from the park.

5. Jijamata Udyan (Byculla Zoo)

Jijamata Udyan, also known as Rani Baug, is Mumbai's oldest public garden, with a small zoo and botanical garden.

It's an excellent choice for families seeking a peaceful respite in the center of the city.

How to Proceed:

Visit the zoo to see a variety of creatures, such as deer, monkeys, and birds. The zoo also includes a museum with a collection of historical items.

Botanical Garden: Take a stroll through the lush greenery and discover the numerous varieties of trees and plants.

Opening hours: 9:30 AM to 6:00 PM daily; closed on Wednesdays.

Entry fee is ₹50 (about $0.60) for adults and ₹25 (approximately $0.30) for youngsters.

How To Get There: The nearest train station is Byculla, which is only a short walk from the park.

These parks and gardens in Mumbai provide a calm getaway from the city's hustle and bustle, allowing visitors to relax, recharge, and appreciate the city's natural beauty.

Chapter 8.

STREET FOOD AND LOCAL CUISINE

Local cuisine

From traditional Maharashtrian cuisine to Parsi specialties and coastal seafood, Mumbai's food scene has something for everyone.

Exploring the city through its food is an immersive experience, with each bite telling a story about the region's history, traditions, and the people who live there.

Must-Try Local Dishes

1. Pav Bhaji.

Pav Bhaji is an iconic Mumbai dish that was formerly a quick supper for mill workers but is now a popular street snack around the city. It is a spicy vegetable mash (bhaji) served with buttered bread rolls (pav). The bhaji is rich and savory, and is typically served with a dab of butter, chopped onions, and a squeeze of lemon. It's a meal that can be found in practically every part of Mumbai, from street vendors to upscale restaurants.

2 Vada Pav

Vada Pav, also known as the "Mumbai Burger," is a simple but tasty snack. It consists of a spicy potato fritter (vada) sandwiched inside a soft bread roll (pav), served with chutney and fried green chilies.

It's a popular snack in Mumbai, with options ranging from roadside vendors to railway stations.

3. Pani Puri

Pani Puri is a traditional Mumbai street snack known for its rush of spices.

It comprises hollow, crispy puris stuffed with spicy tamarind water, chickpeas, potatoes, and chutneys.

It is often consumed in one bite, unleashing a torrent of sour and spicy sensations. Pani Puri stalls may be found around the city and are a must-try for any visitor.

4. Bombil Fry (Bombay Duck) Despite its name, Bombay Duck is actually a sort of fish (Bombil) that lives around Mumbai's coast.

The fish is marinated in spices, covered with semolina, then fried till crispy. It's a popular dish in coastal restaurants, and it pairs well with a squeeze of lime and a cold beverage.

5. Bhel Puri. Bhel puri is a light and pleasant snack made with puffed rice, sev (crispy noodles), chopped onions, tomatoes, and tamarind chutney.

It's the ideal combination of sweet, sour, and spicy flavors, making it a popular choice for a quick snack by the seaside, particularly at Chowpatty Beach.

6. Keema Pav

Keema Pav is a substantial meal of spicy minced meat (often mutton or chicken) eaten with soft bread rolls. It's a popular choice for people looking for a substantial dinner, with many Irani cafés throughout Mumbai dishing up some of the greatest varieties.

7. Modak Modak is a delicious dumpling prepared from rice flour and filled with coconut, jaggery, and almonds. It is especially popular during the Ganesh Chaturthi celebration because it is believed to be Lord Ganesha's favorite dessert.

However, it is available year-round in sweet stores throughout the city.

Recommended Restaurant
1. Leopold Cafe

Location: Colaba Causeway, Colaba, Mumbai.

Cuisine: Continental, Indian, and Chinese.

A historic establishment that has served both residents and tourists since 1871.

It is noted for its lively ambiance, extensive menu, and as the location for Gregory David Roberts' novel "Shantaram.

Opening Hours: 7:30 AM to 12:00 AM.

Cost: Moderate.

Reservation: Not necessary, but recommended during peak hours.

Specials: Chicken Tandoori, Beer Towers, and Hakka Noodles.

2. Britannia & Co.

Location: Ballard Estate, Fort, Mumbai.

Cuisine: Parsi and Indian

This iconic Parsi restaurant provides a memorable dining experience.

The interiors and menu have stayed mostly intact since its inception in 1923.

Opening Hours: 11:30 AM to 4:00 PM (closed on Sundays).

Cost: Moderate.

Reservation: Not required; nevertheless, arrive early to minimize waiting.

Specialties: berry pulav, sali boti, and caramel custard

3. Bombay Canteen

Location: Kamala Mills Compound, Lower Parel, Mumbai.

Cuisine: Modern Indian

This stylish eatery serves a modern twist on traditional Indian meals made using seasonal ingredients.

It is a popular destination for both locals and expats.

Opening Hours: 12:00 PM to 1:00 AM.

Cost: moderate to expensive.

Reservations: Highly recommended, particularly for dinner.

Specials: Kejriwal Toast, Pulled Pork Tacos, and Prawn Lonche.

4. Trishna

Location: Kala Ghoda, Fort, Mumbai

Cuisine: seafood and coastal

Trishna is a seafood lover's dream, known for its Mangalorean coastal cuisine.

The crab dishes are especially popular.

Opening Hours: 11:30 AM - 3:30 PM and 6:30 PM - 12:00 AM.

Cost: Very expensive.

Reservation is highly encouraged, especially on weekends.

Specials: Butter Garlic Crab, Tandoori Prawns, and Neer Dosa.

5. Swati Snacks

Location: Tardeo Road, Tardeo, Mumbai.

Cuisine: vegetarian, Gujarati, street food.

Swati Snacks serves a clean, upscale version of traditional Indian street cuisine, with a focus on vegetarian Gujarati meals.

It's excellent for a quick yet authentic lunch.

Opening Hours: 12:00 PM to 10:30 PM.

Cost: Moderate.

Casual. Reservation: Not accepted; anticipate waiting during peak hours.

Specials: Panki, Sev Puri, and Dahi Batata Puri.

These restaurants are all strategically positioned, making them ideal for tourists visiting Mumbai's top attractions.

Chapter 9.

NIGHTLIFE & ENTERTAINMENT

Bars, Pubs And Clubs

Mumbai's nightlife has something for everyone, whether you want to drink a fine martini, dance till morning, or discover the thriving street food scene. Here's how to make the most of your nights in this thriving metropolis.

Bars and Pubs

1. Aer, Four Seasons Hotel

For those who prefer to drink with a view, Aer at the Four Seasons Hotel is a must-see.

Located on the 34th floor, this open-air bar provides panoramic views of the Mumbai skyline, making it one of the city's most sophisticated locales.

What to Expect:

Extensive menu featuring inventive drinks, great wines, and gourmet appetizers.

Live DJ sets featuring anything from chill-out music to lively songs.

A fashionable, affluent population.

Location: Four Seasons Hotel in Worli.

Entry is free, but reservations are encouraged.

Opening hours: 5:30 p.m. to 1:30 a.m.

Dress Code: Smart casual.

2. The Bombay Canteen

The Bombay Canteen, located in the heart of Lower Parel, is a hip venue noted for its inventive Indian food and unique drinks menu.

It's the ideal setting for a fun evening with friends.

Expect signature cocktails such as the "Desi Whiskey Sour" and craft brews.

A lively atmosphere with vintage decor and a welcoming audience.

A menu that combines traditional Indian flavors with a contemporary twist.

Location: Kamala Mills in Lower Parel.

Opening Hours: 12:00 PM to 1:00 AM.

Dress Code: Casual.

3. Gadda Da Vida

Located at the Novotel in Juhu,

Gadda Da Vida provides a pleasant seaside experience. It's the ideal spot to have a drink while admiring the sunset over the Arabian Sea.

What to Expect: Extensive drink menu focusing on cocktails and spirits.

Outdoor seats with a view of Juhu Beach.

A laid-back atmosphere, perfect for unwinding after a hard day.

Location: Novotel, Juhu Beach.

Entry: Free with early evening happy hours.

Opening hours: 4:00 PM to 1:00 AM.

Dress Code: Smart casual.

Mumbai Nightlife: Bars, Clubs, and Late-Night Activities

1. Tryst

A popular nightclub in Mumbai for dance enthusiasts. Tryst is known for its high-energy environment, stunning light shows, and top-tier DJs, ensuring an amazing night out.

What to Expect:

A lively dance floor with a young crowd.

International and local DJs playing the latest hits.

VIP areas with bottle service for those looking to party in luxury.

Location: High Street Phoenix, Lower Parel.

Entry: ₹2000-₹5000 (about. $24-$60), depending on the event.

Opening hours: 10:00 p.m. to 3:00 a.m.

Dress Code: Club wear.

2. Kitty Su

If you want a more premium nightlife experience, Kitty Su at The Lalit is the place to go.

This high-end club is well-known for its lavish parties, star sightings, and gorgeous clientele.

What to Expect:

Luxurious interior with modern decor and soft chairs. - A music mix featuring EDM, house, and Bollywood sounds.

Themed nights and events with worldwide DJs and musicians.

Location: The Lalit, Andheri East.

Entry Fee: ₹2500-₹7000 (approx. $30-$85), depending on the event.

Opening hours: 10:00 p.m. to 3:00 a.m.

Dress Code: Glamorous and stylish.

3. Colaba Social Offers a laid-back night out with interesting décor, terrific food, and amazing music.

It's popular with both locals and expats, thanks to its relaxed atmosphere and inventive cocktails.

Expect a diverse cuisine with options ranging from burgers to Indian street food.

Signature cocktails include "Long Island Iced Chai" and "Cosmopolitan."

A lively atmosphere featuring live music and special events.

Location: Colaba Causeway, Colaba.

Entry: Free, with reasonable food and beverage costs.

Opening hours: 9:00 a.m. to 1:00 a.m.

Dress Code: Casual.L

The Best Places for a Night Out.

The Mumbai nightlife scene is as diverse as the city itself. When the sun goes down in Mumbai, there's something for everyone, from high-energy nightclubs to relaxing seaside pubs. Whether you want to dance the night away at a high-end club like Kitty Su, sip a refined drink at Aer, or simply unwind with friends at a neighborhood pub like The Bombay Canteen, Mumbai has everything. So put on your best gear, gather your pals, and prepare to enjoy Mumbai's enchantment after dark!

Chapter 10.

FESTIVALS AND EVENTS

Throughout the year, the city is alive with festivities that celebrate its rich legacy and vibrant character. From big religious festivals to cultural extravaganzas, Mumbai always has something going on that will attract both locals and tourists.

Here's a guide to some of Mumbai's most thrilling and colorful events, as well as when to schedule your visit.

1. Ganesh Chaturthi

August or September (dates vary based on Hindu lunar calendar)

What to Expect: Ganesh Chaturthi, Mumbai's largest and most popular holiday, commemorates the birth of Lord Ganesha, the elephant-headed god of wisdom and prosperity.

The city comes alive with colorful decorations, processions, and the sound of devotional music.

Gigantic, intricately carved Ganesha idols are placed in homes and public pandals (temporary stages) and worshiped for ten days.

The event culminates in a grand immersion ritual known as Visarjan, during which the idols are carried to the sea amid much grandeur and chanting.

Tip for Travelers: To fully experience the celebration, visit prominent pandals like Lalbaugcha Raja in Parel or Siddhivinayak Temple in Prabhadevi.

However, be ready for heavy crowds. It's best to dress modestly and follow local customs.

2. Diwali

October or November (dates vary according on Hindu lunar calendar)

Expectations: Diwali, also known as the Festival of Lights, is hugely popular in Mumbai.

The city is lit up with ornamental lights, and homes are decorated with oil lamps (diyas), rangoli (colorful patterns drawn on the floor), and flowers. The air is filled with the sound of fireworks, and sweets are given between relatives and friends. Diwali is also a shopping festival, with many retailers offering tempting discounts and special collections.

Tip for Travelers:

Diwali is an excellent time to enjoy Mumbai's festive vibe.

Visit local markets like Crawford Market or Zaveri Bazaar to experience the shopping frenzy and indulge in traditional delights like ladoos and mithai.

Be cautious of firecrackers and consider seeing the fireworks from a safe distance, such as Marine Drive.

3. Kala Ghoda Arts Festival

February (first week)

What To Expect: The Kala Ghoda Arts Festival is Mumbai's most important cultural festival, held yearly in the bustling Kala Ghoda neighborhood.

This nine-day festival honors the arts in all genres, including visual arts, music, dance, literature, theater, and film.

Streets and venues in the neighborhood are turned into open-air galleries and performance spaces, complete with workshops, exhibitions, and installations that draw artists and art enthusiasts from all over the country.

Tip for Travelers: The festival is free and open to everyone, offering it a fantastic opportunity to experience Mumbai's cultural atmosphere. Because the neighborhood gets congested, it's preferable to visit during the week or early in the mornings. Don't miss the street food stalls, which serve a sample of Mumbai's culinary delicacies.

4. Mumbai International Film Festival (MIFF).

January or February (biannual event)

What To Expect: MIFF is one of Asia's largest film festivals for documentary, short fiction, and animated films.

It provides a platform for filmmakers from all over the world to present their work and engage in discussions about the art and craft of filmmaking.

Screenings are held in a variety of venues throughout the city, including the National Centre for the Performing Arts (NCPA).

Tip for Travelers: If you love movies, MIFF is a must-see event.

Individual screening permits or tickets are available for purchase both online and at the venue. To get a decent seat, check the schedule ahead of time and arrive early.

5. Holi

When: March (day after full moon)

What to Expect: Holi, or the Festival of Colors, is a joyful event that heralds the approach of spring. In Mumbai, people come together to play with colors, water, and traditional sweets.

People of all ages take part in this joyful festival, which transforms the city's streets into a canvas of vibrant colors.

It's a time for celebration, music, and dance.

Tip for Travelers: If you want to participate in the festivities, wear old clothes that you don't mind getting dirty.

Some places conduct scheduled Holi parties with music, food, and organic colors, which may provide a safer and more controlled setting for visitors.

Avoid traveling alone late in the day since the streets can become raucous.

When to Visit Mumbai for the Most Exciting Celebrations?

The finest months to visit Mumbai for its festivals and festivities are October through March.

This time period includes important events such as Diwali, Christmas, New Year's, and the Kala Ghoda Arts Festival.

Furthermore, the weather is generally milder and more pleasant throughout these months, making them perfect for touring and outdoor activities. Whether you want to engage in cultural experiences or simply enjoy the city's festive atmosphere, scheduling your vacation around these events will ensure a great visit to Mumbai.

Theaters and Live Performances

Entertainment center in Mumbai is known for more than Bollywood. The city is a booming center for theater and live entertainment, with a diverse range of drama, dance, music, and comedy that reflects its rich cultural heritage. From famous playhouses to experimental locations, Mumbai's theater culture is as vibrant as the city.

Below is the list of the best theaters and live entertainment places, as well as some useful tourist information.

1.Prithvi Theatre

The Kapoor family, an Indian film dynasty, built one of Mumbai's most famous cultural institutions, the Prithvi Theatre.

Prithvi is known for its small atmosphere and eclectic programming, with performances ranging from classical tragedies to modern plays.

Expect a variety of Hindi, English, and regional language plays.

Regular theater festivals and workshops.

The Prithvi Café is an artsy cafe where you may see actors and artists.

Location: 20 Janki Kutir, Juhu Church Road, Juhu, Mumbai.

Timings: Show times vary; please see the official website for the schedule.

The entry fee is: Ticket costs range from ₹150 to ₹500 (about $2-6).

Booking: Advance reservations are recommended, either online or at the venue.

The nearest train stations are Vile Parle and Santacruz (Western Line).

2. Royal Opera House

The Royal Opera House, India's sole surviving opera house, is an architectural masterpiece and historical landmark.

After undergoing extensive renovations, it reopened as a premier venue for theater, music concerts, and cultural events, combining old-world elegance with modern comforts.

What to Expect:

Luxurious interiors featuring Italianate architecture.

A diverse range of performances, including classical music, drama, and international events.

Special events, such as cinema screenings and art exhibitions.

Location: Mama Parmanand Marg, near Charni Road in Girgaon, Mumbai.

Timings: Show times vary; please see the official website for details.

The entry fee is: Ticket costs vary by event, typically ranging from ₹500 to ₹2,500 (about. $6 to $30).

Booking: Tickets are available for purchase online or at the box office.

Nearest Transportation: Charni Road Railway Station (Western Line).

3. National Centre for the Performing Arts (NCPA)

The NCPA is Mumbai's cultural powerhouse, hosting a varied range of performances in five venues on its premises.

From Indian classical music to contemporary dance and international theater, the NCPA brings together Mumbai's cultural enthusiasts.

What to Expect:

A diverse selection of performances, including Indian and Western classical music, dance, theater, and film screenings.

Annual festivals include the Symphony Orchestra of India and Tata Literature Live!

Performance-related educational programs and workshops.

Location: NCPA Marg, Nariman Point, Mumbai.

Timings: Performance times vary; please check the official website.

Entry Fee: Ticket costs vary per event, ranging from ₹300 to ₹3,000 (about. $4 to $36).

Booking: Tickets can be purchased online, at the NCPA box office, or from approved outlets.

4. St. Andrew's Auditorium

St. Andrew's Auditorium in Bandra, Mumbai's western neighborhood, is a renowned venue for plays, musical events, and stand-up comedy shows. It has about 800 seats and is one of the city's biggest theatrical spaces.

Expect a variety of local theatrical shows, live music, and comedy evenings.

Performances in three languages: English, Hindi, and Marathi.

Conveniently located in the vibrant Bandra district, close to restaurants and cafés.

Location: St. Andrew's College, St. Dominic Road, Bandra West, Mumbai.

Timings: Show times vary; refer to the official schedule.

The entry fee is: Ticket costs often range between ₹200 and ₹1,000 (about. $2.50 to $12).

Booking: Advance reservations are recommended, and they can be made online or at the venue.

Nearest Transportation: Bandra Railway Station (Western Line).

The city's diverse performing scene, which ranges from vast historic venues to intimate independent theaters, reflects its dynamic character and rich cultural legacy. Remember that there is no better keepsake than a recollection of an outstanding live performance!

Chapter 11.
OUTDOOR ACTIVITIES

Beaches

Mumbai's coastline is lined with a variety of beaches, each giving a distinct experience. You may want to relax, eat street food, or watch a beautiful sunset, these beaches offer the ideal escape from the rush and bustle of city life.

Here's an overview of some of Mumbai's most popular beaches:

Juhu Beach

Juhu Beach is a popular Mumbai beach with a bustling vibe.

It's a popular hangout for both locals and tourists, providing a combination of relaxation and entertainment.

As you go along the beach, you'll come across various food carts providing local delicacies such as pav bhaji and bhel puri.

What to See and Do

Enjoy sunset views over the Arabian Sea.

Sample street food from seaside vendors.

Enjoy leisure activities such as horseback riding and camel rides.

Location: Juhu Tara Road, Juhu, Mumbai.

The Best Time to Visit:

Early morning or evening, particularly for sunset views.

Girgaon Chowpatty Beach

Chowpatty Beach is a cultural icon in Mumbai, known for its significance in local events such as Ganesh Chaturthi.

This beach is busy with activity and is popular among families and tourists.

The neighboring Marine Drive adds to the appeal, making for an ideal evening adventure.

What to See and Do

Attend traditional rites and festivals.

Savor snacks such as panipuri and ragda pattice.

Take a leisurely walk down Marine Drive.

Location: Near Marine Drive in South Mumbai.

The Best Time to Visit: In the evening for a more relaxed atmosphere and a busy street food scene.

Aksa Beach

Aksa Beach provides a calm beach experience away from the city's buzz.

This beach is less touristy, making it ideal for individuals seeking to relax and reconnect with nature.

What to See and Do

Explore the uncrowded shoreline.

Enjoy the natural beauty and tranquil atmosphere.

Relax with a book or just listen to the waves.

Location: Aksa Village in Malad West, Mumbai.

The Best Time to Visit: Weekdays to escape the modest weekend crowds.

Versova Beach

Versova Beach is renowned for its clean environment and active fishing community.

The beach has recently grown in popularity as a result of major cleanup efforts, making it an ideal destination for individuals who value a cleaner, better-maintained beach.

What to See and Do

Discover the local fishing community and its activities.

If you're interested in conservation, volunteer with beach cleanups.

Relax and appreciate the peaceful atmosphere compared to Juhu Beach.

Location: Versova, Andheri West, Mumbai.

The Best Time to Visit: Early in the morning or late afternoon.

Madh Island Beach

This quiet hideaway combines beaches, villages, and farms.

It's a bit of a drive from the city, but the peaceful mood and beautiful scenery make the trip worthwhile.

This is the ideal location for a relaxing escape, picnics, or a quiet day by the sea.

What to See and Do

Discover local communities and farms.

Have a relaxing lunch by the beach.

Enjoy the beautiful beauty away from the city's turmoil.

Location: Madh Island in Malad West, Mumbai.

Best Time to Visit: During the day, preferably on weekdays.

Mumbai's beaches provide a welcome respite from the urban scene, with each offering its own distinct appeal. Whether you want a bustling setting with local cuisine or a calm escape, these beaches offer to all tastes.

Trekking and Nature Trails
Water Sports

The city may be a hectic metropolis, but there are plenty of options for nature enthusiasts to escape to the serenity of lush green pathways and stunning scenery.

Whether you're an experienced trekker or a beginner, these hiking and nature routes around Mumbai will leave you feeling rested and invigorated.

1. Sanjay Gandhi National Park

Sanjay Gandhi National Park is a vast green oasis in Mumbai, with paths suitable for all abilities of trekkers. The park is known for its beautiful flora, tranquil lakes, and the historic Kanheri Caves.

What to See and Do:

Visit Kanheri Caves, an ancient Buddhist rock-cut edifice.

Take the Shilonda Trail, which is wonderful for bird watching and butterfly seeing.

Take a relaxing boat ride on the Tulsi Lake.

Location: Borivali East, Mumbai

Entry Fee: ₹58 (approx. $0.70).

Best Time to Visit: For a more green experience, go early in the morning or late in the afternoon, particularly during the rainy season.

Trekking Difficulty: Easy to moderate.

2. Karnala Fort Trek

Karnala Fort provides a moderate trekking experience with panoramic views of the Sahyadri mountain range. The journey is particularly popular among history buffs and nature lovers.

What to See and Do:

Visit the fort's peak to explore historic ruins and admire breathtaking views.

Explore the Karnala Bird Sanctuary, home to over 150 bird species, and observe the diverse flora and animals.

Practical Information:

Location: Panvel, Maharashtra (about 50 kilometers from Mumbai).

Entry fee is ₹30 (about $0.35).

The Best Time to Visit: October through March for beautiful weather.

Moderate trekking difficulty.

3. Matheran

Matheran is a small hill station near Mumbai that is car-free, making it a great site for trekking and nature treks.

The location is noted for its temperate environment, rich flora, and breathtaking views.

What to See and Do:

Visit Panorama Point for stunning sunrise views.

Explore the deep forests by foot or horseback.

Visit Charlotte Lake, which is ideal for a tranquil walk or picnic.

Location: Raigad district, Maharashtra (about 80 kilometers from Mumbai).

The entry fee is ₹50 (about. $0.60) for adults and ₹25 (approx. $0.30) for minors.

Best Time to Visit:

November through February for cool weather.

Trekking Difficulty: Easy to moderate.

Watersports in Mumbai

Adventure seekers can enjoy a variety of water sports along Mumbai's coastline. If you're seeking a thrill or simply want to have a good time, these activities are the ideal way to get away from the daily grind.

1. Jet Skiing at Juhu Beach

Jet skiing is a popular water sport in Juhu Beach that provides an adrenaline-pumping experience as you race across the waves.

What to See and Do:

Ride a jet ski along the coast to experience the wind and waves.

Enjoy the beachside scene, which includes food booths and entertainment.

Location: Juhu Beach in Mumbai.

Cost: ₹500-₹1000 (about. $6-$12) per ride, depending on time.

Best Time to Visit: October to March for calmer waves.

2. Kayaking in Powai Lake

Kayaking Powai Lake provides a relaxing and scenic experience, perfect for those wishing to enjoy water activities in a peaceful setting.

What to See and Do:

Paddle across the tranquil waters of Powai Lake and enjoy the surrounding greenery.

Observe the local birds and appreciate the tranquil setting.

Location: Powai Lake, Mumbai.

Cost: ₹300-₹500 (approx. $4-$6) per hour.

The Best Time to Visit: Early morning or late afternoon for a cooler atmosphere.

3. Scuba Diving in Tarkarli Beach

For those prepared to venture a little further, Tarkarli Beach provides scuba diving chances, allowing you to experience the rich underwater world of the Arabian Sea.

What to See and Do:

Explore the clean seas with coral reefs, colorful fish, and marine life.

Try additional beach activities such as paragliding and banana boat rides.

Location: Tarkarli, Maharashtra (about 500 kilometers from Mumbai).

Cost per dive: ₹1500-₹3000 (approx. $18-$36), including equipment.

For optimal diving conditions, visit between October and February.

The nearest transportation option is Malvan, followed by a short cab journey.

Chapter 12

DAY TRIPS FROM MUMBAI

Elephanta Island

Elephanta Island, a UNESCO World Heritage site, is among the most popular day trips from Mumbai. Located in Mumbai Harbour, this island is well-known for its ancient rock-cut temples devoted to the Hindu god Shiva.

These caves, with their exquisite carvings and enormous sculptures, provide an intriguing look into India's rich cultural legacy.

Getting to Elephanta Island is rather simple, beginning with a lovely ferry trip from the Gateway of India:

Ferry Ride

Location: The ferry to Elephanta Island departs from the Gateway of India in South Mumbai.

Frequency: Ferries run every 30 minutes from 9:00 AM until around 2:00 PM.

Duration: The ferry voyage takes around an hour each way.

Returning Trip: The last ferry from Elephanta Island to Mumbai leaves at 5:30 PM.

Island Accessibility:

Walk: From Elephanta jetty, a 10-15 minute walk leads to the cave complex entrance.

Mini Train: A toy train is offered from the jetty to the base of the hill for a modest price.

Steps: Prepare to climb a set of steps going to the caves. Along the walk, you'll see stalls selling souvenirs, snacks, and beverages.

Cost Summary

1. Ferry Cost:

standard Ferry Ticket: Approximately $2 to $3 (₹150 to ₹200) each round trip.

Deluxe Ferry Ticket: Costs approximately $4 to $5 (₹300 to ₹400) and provides more comfortable sitting options.

2. Entrance Fee:

Foreign Tourists: Around $7 (₹600).

Indian Citizens: Around $0.60 (₹50).

Children (under 15): Free.

3. Toy Train Ride Cost: The cost is approximately $0.10 (₹10) one-way.

4. Guide Services:

Cost: Hiring a local guide for a tour of the caves might cost $6 to $12 (₹500 to ₹1,000), depending on the duration and level of information.

5. Food and souvenirs:Estimated cost: Prices for refreshments and small souvenirs range from $5 to $10 (₹400 to ₹800).

Total Estimated Cost Per Person

Budget Trip: $10 to $12 (₹800 to ₹1000).

The Mid-Range Trip costs $15 to $20 (₹1,200 to ₹1,600) and includes a luxurious ferry, guide service, and snacks.

Important Tip:

Ferry Tickets: Buy your ferry tickets early in the morning to ensure a spot, especially on weekends.

Footwear: Wear comfortable shoes because the steps may be steep and uneven.

Photography: Photographs are permitted, but there is a small fee for using a camera inside the caves.

Water and Snacks: Bring water and snacks as food options on the island may be limited.

Elephanta Island provides an ideal balance of adventure and culture, making it a must-see on any Mumbai itinerary.

Alibaug
A Coastal Escape

Alibaug, known as the "Goa of Maharashtra," is a lovely coastal town near Mumbai. With its stunning beaches, historic forts, and tranquil setting, it's the ideal vacation for people wishing to get away from the city for a day.

Here's how to get the most out of your visit, including accessibility options and pricing.

Getting to Alibaug:

By Ferry: The most popular way to go to Alibaug from Mumbai is by ferry.

Ferries depart from the Gateway of India and take passengers to Mandwa Jetty, from which they can catch a bus or rickshaw to Alibaug.

Regular ferry: $3-$5 (INR 250-INR 400) per person, one way.

Speedboat: $50 to $100 (INR 4,000 to INR 8,000) per boat, one way (may be shared by 6-8 persons).

Trip Time: Regular ferry takes 60-90 minutes.

Speedboat: 20 to 30 minutes.

Departure Location: Gateway of India, Colaba.

Ferry Times: 6:15 AM to 7:00 PM (ferries depart every 30-60 minutes).

Tips: Ferries can be packed on weekends and holidays, so buy your tickets ahead of time.

By road:

Alternatively, you can drive or hire a car to get to Alibaug. The road route provides spectacular views of the coastline and Western Ghats.

Distance: 95 kilometers (around 2.5 to 3 hours by driving).

Private taxi: $40 to $60 (INR 3,000 to INR 5,000) round trip.

Self-drive automobile rental costs $20 to $30 (INR 1,500 to INR 2,500) each day.

Bus: $2-$4 (INR 150-INR 300) per passenger, one way.

Route: Mumbai to Panvel, Pen, and Alibaug.

Tip: Begin early to avoid traffic, particularly on weekends.

What to See and Do In Alibaug

1. Alibaug Beach This is Alibaug's major beach, and it's a nice place to rest or wander.

The beach is famed for its fine sands and views of the Kolaba Fort, which is accessible on foot during low tide.

Activities: Camel and horseback rides.

Water sports (jet skiing and banana boat excursions).

Visit Kolaba Fort (accessible at low tide).

Complete Accessibility

The beach offers flat, sandy ground, making it accessible to everyone.

Tip: To avoid the heat, visit early in the morning or late afternoon.

2. Kolaba Fort. Kolaba Fort, located off the coast, is a medieval stronghold with breathtaking views of the Arabian Sea.

During low tide, you can walk to the fort, but high tide requires a boat journey.

Entry fee is free. - Boat rides cost $1 - $2 (INR 80 - INR 150) each person.

Times: 10:00 AM to 5:00 PM.

Tips: The walk to the fort can be slick, so wear strong shoes.

3. Kihim Beach

Known for its quiet waves and serene setting, Kihim Beach is ideal for people seeking relaxation.

The beach is bordered with coconut trees and provides a peaceful respite from the busier Alibaug Beach.

Activities: Bird watching (ideal for observing migratory birds).

Photography (scenic scenery with fewer people).

Relaxing under the shade of palm trees.

Tip: Bring your own snacks because there are minimal food alternatives.

4. Alibaug's Coastal Cuisine.

Do not leave Alibaug without sampling the local cuisine, especially the fresh seafood.

Several coastal shacks and eateries serve exquisite Malvani cuisine, such as fish curry, fried prawns, and solkadhi.

Recommended Restaurants

Sanman Restaurant: Offers real seafood.

Bohemyan Blue: serves a combination of continental and Indian food.

Meal Cost: $5-$15 (INR 400-INR 1,200) per person.

A day excursion to Alibaug from Mumbai allows you to relax and enjoy the natural beauty and history of this coastal town.

Lonavala and Khandala

Escape the city's hustle and bustle with a rejuvenating day trip to the picturesque hill stations of Lonavala and Khandala.

Just a few hours from Mumbai, these twin places provide stunning views, rich foliage, and the ideal balance of rest and adventure.

Getting there

1. By Car:

Duration: Around 2 hours (83 km)

Cost: INR 1,500-2,500 ($20-$30) for gasoline and tolls.

Flexible schedule, increased comfort, and the freedom to explore at your own leisure.

2. Train:

Duration: 2-2.5 hours from Mumbai to Lonavala.

Cost: INR 150–400 ($2-$5) per person, depending on the type of travel.

Economical and scenic, with many trains running throughout the day.

3. Bus ride:

Duration: 2.5-3 hours.

The cost is INR 200-500 ($3-$6) per person.

Regular services available from Mumbai, but less flexible than driving.

Lonavala and Khandala are both accessible to all types of travelers, including those with mobility problems. Some sights, such as Lonavala Lake and Bhushi Dam, are wheelchair accessible, but it is recommended to have help owing to difficult terrain in some parts.

Things to See and Do

1. Lonavala Lake:

A quiet area excellent for a morning stroll or boat ride. - Wheelchair accessible, however some assistance is required on uneven paths.

Entry Fee: Free.

2. Bhushi Dam:

Popular for its cascading rivers, especially during the monsoon.

Some portions may be difficult for persons with mobility impairments, especially during the rainy season when the terrain is slick.

Entry Fee: Free.

3. Karla Caves:

Buddhist carvings in ancient rock-cut caves.

Moderate trek up the hill, not suitable for individuals with mobility issues.

Entry Fee: INR 25 ($0.30) for Indians, INR 300 ($3.70) for foreign tourists.

4. Tiger's Leap:

A cliff-top with panoramic views of the valley.

Easily accessible by road, with viewing locations for all tourists.

Entry Fee Free.

5. Rajmachi Point:

Provides breathtaking views of the Rajmachi Fort and adjacent valleys.

Car-accessible with viewing spaces for all visitors. - Entry Fee: Free.

Trip Cost Summary

Transportation Options

Car: INR 1,500-2,500 ($20-$30)

Train: INR 150-400 ($2-$5) per person

Bus: INR 200-500 ($3-$6) per person

Food & Beverage:

Estimated Cost: INR 500-1,000 ($6-$12) per person, based on dining options.

Attractions:

Total Entry Fees: Approximately INR 325-650 ($4-$8) per person, including Karla Caves.

Total Estimated Cost:

For a Solo Traveler: INR 2,475 to 4,150 ($30-50) based on transportation and eating options.

For a Family of Four: INR 7,900-12,000 ($95-$150), which includes travel, food, and attraction entry costs.

The Best Time to Visit

Ideal months for good weather are October through March.

The monsoon season (June to September) provides lush scenery but may present difficulties owing to slippery conditions.

What to pack

Essentials: Bring comfortable walking shoes, a hat, sunscreen, a water bottle, and light snacks.

Monsoon-Specific: Rain gear (umbrella, raincoat), waterproof shoes, and a small towel.

Local transportation options include auto-rickshaws and taxis. Local transportation between Lonavala and Khandala is readily available, as is the opportunity to visit adjacent sights.

Safety Tips:

Monsoon Warnings: Roads can be treacherous, particularly near waterfalls and dams.

Stick to the authorized walkways and wear proper footwear.

Health Status: Carry any prescriptions you may need as well as a tiny first-aid kit.

A day excursion to Lonavala and Khandala provides an ideal balance of nature, history, and relaxation. .

Chapter 13.

ITINERARY

Mumbai Three-Days Itinerary for Solo Travelers

As a lone traveler, you can explore the city at your leisure, discovering hidden gems and famous monuments.

This three-day itinerary is designed to show you the best of Mumbai, with a mix of must-see attractions and local experiences.

Day One: Exploring South Mumbai

Morning: Gateway of India and Colaba.

Begin your day with Mumbai's most recognizable monument, the Gateway of India.

Arrive early to appreciate the tranquil views of the Arabian Sea and take photos without crowds.

Open 24/7; free access.

The Colaba Causeway: Explore Colaba Causeway, a lively market street where you can purchase souvenirs, clothes, and jewelry. Do not forget to bargain!

Late morning: Chhatrapati Shivaji Maharaj Vastu Sangrahalaya.

Visit this museum, formerly known as the Prince of Wales Museum, to learn about Mumbai's rich history, art, and culture.

The museum's Indo-Saracenic architecture is equally impressive.

Open from 10:15 a.m. to 6:00 p.m.; an entry fee applies.

Afternoon Activities: Marine Drive and Chowpatty Beach

Marine Drive: Stroll down Marine Drive, commonly known as the Queen's Necklace due to its crescent form and glittering lights at night.

This beachfront promenade is ideal for a leisurely stroll and boasts breathtaking views of the city skyline.

Chowpatty Beach: Finish the afternoon at Chowpatty Beach, where you can relax on the sand and eat Mumbai's famous street food, such as bhel puri and pav bhaji.

Evening Dinner at a Local Eatery Go to a neighboring restaurant or café for dinner.

South Mumbai has a range of dining alternatives, ranging from traditional Indian food to international fare.

Consider eating at Leopold Café or Café Mondegar for a taste of history and flavor.

Day Two: Culture and Heritage Morning activities include Dhobi Ghat and Haji Ali Dargah.

Begin your morning by going to Dhobi Ghat, the world's largest open-air laundromat.

Watching the dhobis at work provides a unique perspective on Mumbai's daily life.

Open 24/7; free access.

Haji Ali Dargah: Next, go to Haji Ali Dargah, a mosque and tomb located on an islet in the Arabian Sea. It's a peaceful location, especially during low tide, when the causeway is accessible.

Open from 5:30 a.m. to 10:00 p.m.; free admission.

Late Morning at Mani Bhavan Visit Mani Bhavan, Mahatma Gandhi's former house in Mumbai.

This museum provides a moving look into Gandhi's life and efforts during the campaign for Indian freedom.

Open from 9:30 a.m. to 6:00 p.m.; free admission.

Afternoon activities: Crawford Market and Kalbadevi

Crawford Market: Explore Crawford Market, one of Mumbai's oldest markets, where you can buy fresh vegetables, spices, and unique things. It's an excellent site to enjoy the local market vibe.

Open from 11:00 a.m. to 8:00 p.m., closed on Sundays.

Kalbadevi: Wander through the adjacent Kalbadevi area, which is famed for its small streets, vibrant marketplaces, and medieval temples.

Evening: Bandra–Worli Sea Link Take a trip across the Bandra-Worli Sea Link, an engineering marvel that connects South Mumbai and the western suburbs.

The sea link provides amazing views, particularly around sunset.

Day Three: Modern Mumbai and Beyond

Morning in Bandra

Bandra Fort: Begin your day in Bandra, Mumbai's lively suburb.

Visit Bandra Fort, a historic Portuguese fort with spectacular views of the Bandra-Worli Sea Link and the Arabian Sea.

Open from 6:00 a.m. to 7:30 p.m.; free admission.

Street Art in Bandra: Explore Bandra's street art and murals, especially in the Ranwar Village area.

The vibrant artwork celebrates Mumbai's metropolitan culture and innovation.

Late Morning at Siddhivinayak Temple

Visit the Siddhivinayak Temple, which is one of Mumbai's most famous temples and dedicated to Lord Ganesha.

The temple draws thousands of visitors, particularly on Tuesdays.

Open from 5:30 a.m. to 9:50 p.m.; free admittance (donations appreciated).

Afternoon at Juhu Beach Visit Juhu Beach, one of Mumbai's most popular beaches, located in the western suburbs.

The beach is famous for its bustling environment, street food kiosks, and celebrity sightings.

Evening Bollywood Tour

Finish your journey with a Bollywood tour. Mumbai is the core of India's film industry, and various tour firms provide behind-the-scenes visits to film studios.

It's a fantastic way to end your journey, especially if you're a movie fan.

This three-day tour offers a comprehensive overview of Mumbai's many features, from historic landmarks to modern attractions. Enjoy your single voyage in this vibrant metropolis, where every corner holds a fresh story to explore.

Three-Days Itinerary for family visit

Day 1: Exploring the City's Iconic Landmarks

Morning:

1. Gateway of India

Start your day at this iconic landmark. Enjoy the view of the Arabian Sea and take some family photos. - Consider a quick boat ride to see the Gateway from the water.

2. Chhatrapati Shivaji Maharaj

Vastu Sangrahalaya (Prince of Wales Museum)

Visit this museum for a mix of history, art, and culture. The kids will enjoy the impressive collections and the beautiful garden.

Lunch: Leopold Café A historic and family-friendly spot near Colaba Causeway. Enjoy Indian and Continental dishes.

Afternoon:

3. Chhatrapati Shivaji Maharaj Terminus (CST)

Visit this UNESCO World Heritage site.

The architecture is stunning, and it's a great spot for a family photo.

4. Marine Drive & Girgaum Chowpatty Beach

Stroll along Marine Drive, also known as the Queen's Necklace. Let the kids play on the sandy beach at Girgaum Chowpatty.

Enjoy street food like bhel puri or pav bhaji from local vendors.

Evening:

5. Taraporewala Aquarium

Explore Mumbai's oldest aquarium.

The colorful marine life will fascinate children.

6. Nariman Point

End the day with a view of the sunset from Nariman Point, at the end of Marine Drive.

Dinner: Pizza by the Bay

A family-friendly spot offering pizzas and other continental dishes with a sea view.

Day 2: Cultural and Fun Experiences

Morning: 1. Sanjay Gandhi National Park

Take a morning trip to this lush park.

Enjoy a family safari, visit the Kanheri Caves, or take a leisurely boat ride.

There's a mini train ride inside the park that's fun for kids.

Lunch:

Aroma's Café & Bistro (Borivali)

A relaxed place to enjoy a meal before heading to the next attraction.

Afternoon:

2. Global Vipassana Pagoda

Visit this peaceful and beautiful meditation dome near the park. It's a serene spot that the whole family can appreciate.

3. EsselWorld & Water Kingdom

Spend the afternoon at one of India's largest amusement and water parks. There are rides and attractions suitable for all ages.

Evening:

4. Juhu Beach

Head to Juhu Beach in the evening.

Enjoy the local street food, fly kites, and let the kids enjoy the beach atmosphere.

Don't miss out on the famous Juhu chaat.

Dinner:

The Pasta Bar Veneto (Juhu)

A family-friendly restaurant serving Italian cuisine.

Day 3: Local Flavors and Shopping

Morning:

1. Mani Bhavan Gandhi Museum

Start with a visit to the house where Mahatma Gandhi stayed during his visits to Mumbai.

It's educational and interesting for older children.

2. Hanging Gardens and Kamla Nehru Park

These are great spots for a relaxed morning.

The kids will enjoy the shoe-shaped structure in Kamla Nehru Park.

Lunch:

Swati Snacks (Tardeo)

Enjoy a variety of traditional Indian snacks and meals in a clean, family-friendly environment.

Afternoon:

3. Nehru Planetarium

A fun and educational experience for the entire family. The planetarium offers shows about space and the universe.

4. Nehru Science Centre Visit this nearby interactive science museum. It's a great place for children to engage in fun learning activities.

Evening:

5. Crawford Market

Explore this vibrant market with a mix of local produce, spices, and more.

It's a great place to experience local life.

6. Colaba Causeway

A bustling street market where you can shop for souvenirs, clothes, and trinkets. The colorful atmosphere is sure to entertain the kids.

Dinner:

Bademiya (Colaba)

End your day with delicious kebabs and rolls from this famous eatery.

There are seating options nearby for a family meal.

This itinerary balances sightseeing, cultural experiences, and fun activities, making sure there's something for every member of the family to enjoy in Mumbai.

Chapter 14.

PRACTICAL TIPS FOR TRAVELERS

Money and Currency

Understanding money and currency in Mumbai is essential for a good travel experience. Here's a full summary to prepare you for the greatest stay:

Currency:

The Indian Rupee (INR) is the official currency, represented by the symbol ₹. Banknotes are issued in denominations of ₹2,000, ₹500, ₹200, ₹100, ₹50, ₹20, ₹10, and ₹5. Coins have denominations of ₹1, ₹2, ₹5, and ₹10.

Currency Exchange:

Travelers can convert foreign currency at airports, authorized money changers in tourist areas and hotels, or banks (though rates may be less favorable).

Tip: Avoid exchanging in hotels or illegal dealers, as the rates may be much lower.

Recommended Exchange Locations:

Orient Exchange offers cheap prices and many locations in Mumbai.

BookMyForex enables online booking and doorstep delivery of exchanged currencies. Thomas Cook provides trustworthy services in convenient places.

Using ATMs:

ATMs are readily available in urban and tourist regions. International cards bearing the Visa, Mastercard, or Maestro logos are frequently accepted.

Inform your bank about your travel plans to avoid having transactions halted.

Check your bank's ATM withdrawal costs to avoid surprises.

Cashless Transactions:

UPI apps like Paytm and Google Pay are widely utilized for daily purchases in Mumbai, making digital payments more prevalent. Major credit cards are accepted at many shops and eateries. Carrying some cash is still suggested for little transactions and emergencies.

The Cost of Living:

Mumbai is less expensive than other large cities, with economical street food and local transportation. Accommodation and tourism activities differ in price depending on your preferences.

Budgeting Tip:

Create a daily budget and track your costs.

Use public transit for cost-effective travel.

Shop in local markets, particularly for souvenirs.

Choose street food or budget-friendly establishments for meals.

Participate in free activities such as visiting parks and museums.

Language and Communication

Language and communication in Mumbai reflect the city's multicultural and cosmopolitan character. Mumbai's linguistic environment reflects the city's multinational populace. Here's a summary of language and communication in Mumbai:

1. Multilingual Environment: Mumbai's diverse linguistic environment reflects its multiculturalism. Marathi is the official language of Maharashtra, however due to the inflow of people from other regions, a variety of languages are spoken.

2. Marathi: Marathi is the primary language in Mumbai and Maharashtra. It is commonly used in formal communication, education, and everyday life. The city boasts a rich Marathi literary and cultural tradition.

3. Hindi: - Hindi is another widely spoken language, particularly in daily life and the entertainment industry. It acts as a lingua franca, bridging communication gaps between persons with diverse linguistic backgrounds.

4. English: English is widely utilized in commerce, education, and administration. Many schools and institutions use it as their primary medium of education. Furthermore, Mumbai is a financial and commercial hub, thus English is essential for professional communication.

5. Gujarati: With a large Gujarati presence in Mumbai, Gujarati is extensively spoken in specific regions and has a cultural impact, particularly in business and trade.

6. Mumbai has communities speaking Konkani, Tamil, Kannada, Telugu, and Malayalam, representing several South Indian states. As a result, several populations speak languages such as Konkani, Tamil, Kannada, Telugu, and Malayalam.

7. Urdu: Muslims speak Urdu, which has historical and cultural significance. It is also employed in a variety of cultural contexts, including poetry and literature.

8. Bambaiya Hindi or Mumbaiya Hindi:

Bambaiya Hindi, or Mumbaiyya Hindi, is a colloquial and regional variety of Hindi spoken in Mumbai. It combines elements from Marathi, Gujarati, and English to create a distinct linguistic taste.

9. Mumbai has unique street slang and lingo influenced by its fast-paced lifestyle, multiculturalism, and entertainment sector. This informal language distinguishes local conversation.

10. Communication challenges: While linguistic diversity is a positive, it can also create communication barriers. However, Mumbaikars are noted for their versatility, and they frequently transition between languages to efficiently communicate.

11. Signage and Public Communication: - Public signage, government communication, and commercial businesses sometimes use various languages, such as Marathi, Hindi, and English, to reach a varied audience.

Here are some useful phrases for travelers in Mumbai:

1. Greetings:

   - Hello: Namaste (used for both formal and informal greetings)

   - Hi: Hi

   - Good morning: Shubh prabhat

   - Good evening: Shubh sandhya

2. Polite Expressions:

- Please: Kripaya

- Thank you: Dhanyavaad

- Excuse me: Kshama karein

- I'm sorry: Mujhe maaf karo

3. Asking for Help:

- Can you help me?: Kya aap meri madad kar sakte hain?

- Where is...?: ...kahan hai?

- I'm lost: Main kho gaya/gayi hoon

4. Directions:

- Left: Bayen

- Right: Daaye

- Straight ahead: Seedha

- Where is the nearest...?: Sabse nazdik ... kahan hai?

5. Transportation:

- How much is this/that?: Ye/woh kitne ka hai?

- Where is the bus/train station?: Bus/Train station kahan hai?

- How much is a ticket to...?: ...ka ticket kitna hai?

6. Ordering Food:

- I would like…: Mujhe … chahiye

- What is this?: Ye kya hai?

- The bill, please: Bill, kripaya

7. Numbers:

- 1: Ek

- 2: Do

- 3: Teen

- 4: Char

- 5: Paanch

- 10: Das

8. Emergency Situations:

- Help!: Bachao!

- I need a doctor: Mujhe doctor ki zarurat hai

- Where is the nearest hospital?: Sabse nazdik hospital kahan hai?

9. Shopping:

- How much does this cost?: Ye kitne ka hai?

- I would like to buy…: Main … kharidna chahta/chahti hoon

- Do you accept credit cards?: Kya aap credit cards lete hain?

10. Common Expressions:

   - Yes: Haan

   - No: Nahi

   - I don't understand: Mujhe samajh nahi aaya

   - What is your name?: Aapka naam kya hai?

   - My name is...: Mera naam ...

Remember, locals appreciate when visitors make an effort to use local phrases, even if it's just a few words. It can enhance your cultural experience and make your interactions more pleasant.

Health and Medical Services

When visiting Mumbai, it's crucial to be aware of the healthcare alternatives accessible.

Here's a guide to the essential health and medical services you may require during your visit:

Hospitals and Clinics

Kokilaben Dhirubhai Ambani Hospital (Andheri): One of Mumbai's finest multispecialty hospitals, delivering 24-hour emergency treatment.

Lilavati Hospital (Bandra): Known for its advanced medical facilities and knowledgeable staff.

Bombay Hospital (Marine Lines): A well-known hospital in South Mumbai that provides comprehensive medical care.

Hiranandani Hospital (Powai) is well-known for its cutting-edge infrastructure and medical services.

Emergency Services: Most major hospitals in Mumbai offer 24-hour emergency rooms. In the event of an emergency, dial 108 to summon an ambulance.

Pharmacies Availability

Pharmacies are easily accessible throughout Mumbai, with several open 24/7. In addition to huge businesses such as Apollo Pharmacy and Wellness Forever, there are smaller, community drugstores.

Medication: Most common prescriptions are readily available, but it is advisable to bring any prescription medications you may require for the duration of your vacation.

Always retain a copy of your prescriptions while purchasing drugs.

Pharmacists can typically help you with over-the-counter medications for minor conditions.

International Health Insurance

It is advisable to get travel insurance that covers medical situations. Many hospitals in Mumbai accept international insurance, but you should check with your provider before visiting.

Consult your insurance provider for a list of network hospitals in Mumbai. Keep emergency numbers available.

Emergency Contact Information

Ambulance: 108

Police: 100

Fire: 101

Medical assistance is available 24/7.

Practical Tips for Travelers

Carry a basic first-aid kit with bandages, antiseptic wipes, pain relievers, and any necessary medications.

Stay Hydrated: Mumbai's heat and humidity can be extreme, so drink plenty of water to stay hydrated.

Know Your Location: Keep a list of nearby hospitals and pharmacies at your hotel for easy access in the event of an emergency.

Staying knowledgeable about the health and medical services available will help you have a safe and pleasurable vacation to Mumbai.

CONCLUSION

As we come to the end of our adventure through the bustling, chaotic, and completely enthralling city of Mumbai, I hope you're feeling as eager to explore as ever. From the moment you set foot in this city, you'll be swept up in its distinct rhythm—a fusion of history, culture, and pure vibrancy that distinguishes Mumbai.

We've traveled together to see prominent locations such as the magnificent Gateway of India and the tranquil Hanging Gardens.

You've seen how Mumbai's skyline tells the narrative of its colonial history and aspirational future in a single glimpse.

We've visited the crowded markets, where haggling is as much a tradition as the items themselves. Let us not forget the cuisine—oh, the food! From spicy street snacks like pani puri to sumptuous biryanis that would put you in a food coma, Mumbai is a city where every meal is a journey. Just make sure to pack some flexible pants—you'll thank me later!

We've also explored Mumbai's cultural heartbeat, visiting temples, mosques, and churches, each with a unique narrative to share. Mumbai has something for every traveler, whether they are history buffs, foodies, or beach lovers. And, let's be honest: where else can you go from a centuries-old fort to a cutting-edge shopping mall in the same day? As you shut this handbook and ready to embark on your own Mumbai trip, remember that the true enchantment of this city is its ability to surprise you at every turn.

Yes, you'll encounter the famed traffic, but that's all part of the experience—another chance to take in the sights and sounds of everyday life. And if you get lost in the maze of streets, don't worry—you're only one friendly local away from discovering a new favorite spot.

So here's to Mumbai, a city as unpredictable as it is memorable. Dive into the turmoil, embrace the culture, and, most importantly, enjoy every moment. Until our paths cross again, mercy journey!

Printed in Dunstable, United Kingdom